THOUGHTS and NOTES on the ISSUES of RECONCILIATION of WORK and FAMILY LIFE in EUROPE.

The EXPERIENCE of CYPRUS

Maria Gasouka
and Maria Kokkinou

iUniverse, Inc.
New York   Bloomington

THOUGHTS and NOTES on the ISSUES of
RECONCILIATION of WORK and FAMILY LIFE in EUROPE.
The EXPERIENCE of CYPRUS

iUniverse books may be ordered through booksellers or by contacting:

iUniverse
1663 Liberty Drive
Bloomington, IN 47403
www.iuniverse.com
1-800-Authors (1-800-288-4677)

Because of the dynamic nature of the Internet, any Web addresses or links contained in this book may have changed since publication and may no longer be valid. The views expressed in this work are solely those of the author and do not necessarily reflect the views of the publisher, and the publisher hereby disclaims any responsibility for them.

ISBN: 978-1-4502-3273-9 (sc)
ISBN: 978-1-4502-3274-6 (ebk)

Printed in the United States of America

iUniverse rev. date: 06/09/2010

CONTENTS

Introduction

The entry of women into the labor market, the increase of the female labor force and the improvement of the position of many women in the professional hierarchy in the last years constitute factors that steadily undermine the gender distribution of roles and its traditional interdependences. Indubitably, the involvement of women in the modern economic production with the paid professional employment upsets the fine established balance between the private – female space and the public – male one. Female liberalization in the working and social field is linked – according to the modern feminist thought – to the overstepping of the dominant ideology of genders and their social, cultural differences, the refusal of the ideas of natural destination and the rupture vis-à-vis any division between male – female, culture – nature, society – family.

While, however, women are actively integrating in the production process and participate equally in the struggle for a living with their partners[1], we do not see a proportional participation of men in the household responsibilities. Men as a rule are relieved of laborious and time-consuming family obligations such as care, bringing up the children, and elderly parents, as well as dealing with the household chores. They focus on their professional career and success, having as a result to gain more often than women responsible and hierarchically superior posts. On the opposite women in their effort to meet up sufficiently to everything that has been established and named as "family duties" –

which are translated in self-evident female unpaid housework – are de facto oriented to seeking other forms of work (e.g. part-time, short time etc.), which does not have the perspective of social reward, professional development and career with ambitious goals, and sometimes they withdraw (abandon) from the production process. It is not by chance that the female population is often driven to this solution of flexible forms of work and short time since this gives the possibility to combine paid work with the unpaid family work, which the coercions of the patriarchic society render "compulsory" for women (Anker, 1997).

So, taking into consideration all the above information we can say that the relation between family and work covers a dimension which is deeply social, cultural, financial and political. .

Today equality between men and women in all policies constitutes an integral part of the social policy of the European Union and is recognized as a critical factor to its social cohesion and its growth, according to the findings of the European Foundation for the Improvement of Living and Working Conditions, "Quality of Life in Europe" survey (2003). Gender inequality is considered to exercise direct discrimination in the participation of workers, in the fertility, the creation of a family and the quality of life. Issues such as working time, working conditions, lifelong learning, the benefits of the public sector – such as child care and the retirement system – contribute to forming measures with the aim to better balance work and family life for all European citizens.

The reconciliation of family and professional life is a new policy that comes to meet a certain social need, which emerged quite some time ago. By the term reconciliation/harmonisation of family and professional life we mean that it is imperative for both men and women in the contemporary social, economic and cultural circumstances to assume multiple roles as employees, home- and family caretakers and these roles can no longer continue to conflict with each other. The reconciliation of family and professional life can also be expressed as the *balance of professional and family obligations.* The new term refers to the balanced, equivalent participation of both men and women in

Thoughts and Notes on the Issues of Reconciliation
of Work and Family Life in Europe.

ix

family responsibilities in such a way that they are allowed to meet their professional obligations, but also to optimise their creativity and skills at the work place (Dex, Smith & Winter, 2001). The couple's shared responsibility in the family and household tasks and equal opportunities for the two sexes at the work place, which will contribute to their professional evolution, are preconditions for the implementation of this new policy, which has come to complement and forward the gender mainstreaming policy. The gender-based occupational segregation that is prevalent to this day is no longer functional. For women that are traditionally burdened with the household care, the participation in paid labour is not only a wish but also a psychological and economic need. Women's labour is necessary for both improving the living conditions of the family and also the progress of economy and achievement of social cohesion. It is for this reason that there is a formulation of political objectives for raising women's participation in labour. As a consequence, women's entrance to professional life and often (despite the obstacles they face because of their sex) in positions of increased responsibility, the demographic changes, the change of roles of men and women in the family and at work, the emergence of different models of employment are factors that urge the creation of legislation and the adoption of positive measures for the protection of family, as well as its combination with the professional life of both parents, but mostly women (Den & Den, 2001). Positive measures are the *"measures providing for specific advantages in order to make it easier for the underrepresented sex to pursue a vocational activity or to prevent or compensate for disadvantages in professional careers, with a view to ensuring full equality in practice between men and women in working life"* as provided by paragraph 4, article 141 of the Treaty Establishing the European Community (2002)[2].

The recently modernised institutional framework of the Republic of Cyprus provides important provisions that contribute to the possibility of reconciliation of family and professional life of the working people, especially women[3]. However, the need for this reconciliation should by realised by the society, which like other Mediterranean countries (and not only those) still has strong patriarchal reflexes especially in the employing world. To this direction the National Mechanism for Women's Rights take action, as well as institutions of equality like the Equality Observatory of Cyprus, the innovative Women's Cooperative Bank, but also women's departments of the political parties and federations of labour. An important objective of this effort is the information/ sensitisation/encouragement of Cypriot businesses to assume their social role and to contribute to the achievement of this goal, by forming an internal business environment free of prejudices and stereotypes related to the sexes, friendly to women and family in general. An important tool to this direction are today the experiences, good practices and products that resulted from the actions developed in the frame of C.I. EQUAL, mainly by Development Partnerships "Elani" and "Pandora".

NOTES

1. Of course we are talking about women who finally manage to find employment, because we should not forget that the large majority of the unemployed and long-term unemployed people in Europe are women. Thus the question of studying the living conditions of these women remains, as well as their ability to access the systems of social security.

2. The Treaty article 141, paragraph 3, empowers the Community to adopt measures in order to ensure the application of equal treatment of men and women in matters of employment and occupation, whereas Treaty article 141, paragraph 4 aims at defining terms, reinforce protection of individuals lodging complaints, clarify the scope of exemption from certain principles, boost positive action measures to promote equality and safeguard special protection for women on grounds of pregnancy and maternity (Economic and Social Committee, 2001).

3. National policies should focus more on the establishment of a supporting institutional framework that would help lighten the negative consequences that implementation of flexible labour forms and to ensure a greater control on time management to individuals working under these conditions (Mouriki, 2004).

PART I

The European experience

CHAPTER 1.
THE EUROPEAN STRATEGIES
ON EQUALITY.

1.1. *The European labour market from a gender perspective*

The increased rates of development and competitiveness of the European market, the pursuit of social cohesion, the quality itself of the western type democracy have pointed out the fundamental necessity of women's entrance to the labour market and their stay in it, on terms of equality and equal opportunities as it has been pointed out. Female liberalization in the working and social field is linked – according to the modern feminist thought – to the overstepping of the dominant ideology of genders and their social, cultural differences, the refusal of the ideas of natural destination and the rupture vis-à-vis any division between male – female, culture – nature, society – family.

Despite this widely accepted finding, however, women's relation to paid labour and self-employment is characterised by a network of prejudices and notions connected to traditionally patriarchal relevant attitudes, resulting in facing serious obstacles in their evolution and career. Briefly approaching the labour market from the point of view of gender, it is realised that along with the changes in economic and social circumstances, in the past three decades women enter the labour market at a constantly increasing rate (Montana & Charnov, 2000). Despite that, throughout the E.U. there have been sex discriminations in the areas of both paid and unpaid labour. Women in the Community are still the majority of those employed with "flexible" forms of work[1], of the unemployed and the long-term unemployed. They are still paid less for work of the same quality, time and qualifications, they face the "glass ceiling" in their professional evolution and they are underrepresented in the centres of economic, political and social decision making. Occupational segregation in male and female professions is still visible, as well as women's professional immobility and limited presence in informal forms of employment, etc. It is also known that women comprise the largest part of the unemployed and the long-term unemployed in the majority of the European countries. Furthermore, there is an uneven distribution of men and women in professions, fields and forms of employment. Men usually occupy positions of authority, with the highest salary in relation to women (uneven access), who are the first to suffer the consequences of any economic crises. In general the gender dimension of the European labour market is specified as such:

1. In almost all member states the rate of unemployed women remains systematically higher than that of men, whereas women are the ones to suffer long-term unemployment more.
2. The difference in the rate of employment between men and women is about 20%.
3. Women's rate of employment is reduced when they have children, while the opposite stands for men.

The occupational segregation of men and women in the labour market remains a critical problem for the European Union. Even countries where women have achieved high rates of employment demonstrate segregated professional structures. Women's salary is lower than that of men for the same or same value work, a fact of wide dimensions in Cyprus, where the difference rate is about 25%. The difference in salary is higher in the private sector than in the public one, whereas

Thoughts and Notes on the Issues of Reconciliation
of Work and Family Life in Europe.

5

structural factors such as age, profession and field of activity do not seem to contribute to the reduction in salary difference. Finally, the limitation of traditionally "female" professions by the introduction of new technologies renders women's professional training/re-specialisation immediately necessary, so that they are able to respond to the demands of the new work positions.

Gender-based occupational segregation stems from the socialisation process of the sexes, the limitations women face regarding paid labour – gender-based division of household labour or a social state based on the family model of the male bread winner and the dependent wife (Gasouka, 2007). Thus, there is a vertical segregation that minimises women's possibilities of assuming managerial positions, a horizontal segregation in the fields of employment depending on a person's sex and inequalities in salary that still exist, despite the fact that the European Union has a long tradition in the regulation of equal salaries (European Foundation for the Improvement in Living and Working Conditions, 2000). At the same time, while women actively enter the productive process and participate as much as their husbands in earning a living, there is not a similar participation of men in the household responsibilities. By rule, men are free of hard, time-consuming responsibilities such as caring, keeping and upbringing children and elderly parents, as well as involvement in household tasks. They focus on their professional career and success, with the result of assuming responsible, higher positions earlier than women (Griswold, 1993)[2]. On the other hand, in their effort to adequately respond to the so-called "family duties" (translated into implicit unpaid household labour), women seek forms of employment that have no prospect of social recognition, professional evolution, a career with ambitious goals (Kaklamanaki, 1984), or they even exit the productive process. The female population is often forced to this necessity solution of reduced working hours, because it gives them the opportunity to combine paid labour with unpaid domestic work, which is rendered "obligatory" for women by the constraints of the patriarchal society (Avramikou, 2001).

In the late 1990s the measures regarding the rearrangement of working time (part-time employment, long parental leaves, flexible hours, etc.) were given a lot of emphasis aiming at the flexibility of the labour market. This emphasis however, especially when it is addressed mainly to women despite the official rhetoric, has negative effects on equal opportunities in the labour market. As it appeared, it leads back to the traditional roles of the sexes and has negative implications to women's professional evolution. In the end these forms do not support women's efforts in entering the labour market and competing with men on equal terms. At the same time, men experience interpersonal and internal conflicts within the family because of an already visible contradiction between the older "paternal role" according to which they have been raised and to the new roles and attitudes they are called for to adopt by contemporary needs (Gasouka, 2007). Nowadays it is widely accepted that the redistribution of social roles inside the family, the transformation of biological motherhood into a social one with both parents' participation in children's upbringing is a historical – social necessity (Lupton & Barclay, 1997).

Consequently, the issue of equal opportunities to labour is raised immediately. At the same time, women's increased participation in employment, but also the important changes in family models that led to an increased number of nuclear and single-parent families, created a stronger need for a reconciliation of family and professional life (Mouriki, 2005). The combination of conflicting demands between paid labour and family needs and tasks is acknowledged as a great challenge for employees of every field and especially women, whose responsibilities are traditionally raised in the sphere of the home[3]. Either way, this family model, where both parents work and has been the European rule in the last decade with its socio-cultural turns, creates stress and tension to its members because of the conflicting demands of family and work (O'Brien & Shelmit, 2003).

Thoughts and Notes on the Issues of Reconciliation
of Work and Family Life in Europe.

7

Table 1: Weekly involvement (work hours) in households where two parents with dependent children have a full-time employment, 2000.

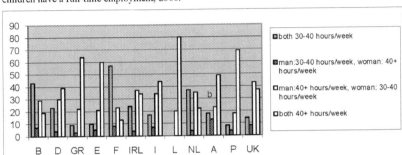

Source: LFS 2000, IRL: 1997; L and UK: 1999; DK, FIN and S: no data.

Two needs emerge: on one hand parents, especially women, need to have enough time both for their children and other family members that may require care from time to time, and themselves [4]. We should not forget that there is also an issue of redistributing family time in favour of the women too, which is often completely neglected. On the other hand, it is important that preschool and school children enjoy high quality care, which has proved to be of particular significance for the development of their cognitive and psychological abilities (Kokkinou, 2008). Unfortunately, the inability to combine these roles is experienced in a culpatory way by parents, especially women that regard themselves the principal caretakers of the family.

According to the proposals of the European Committee and the social partners, the first need can be met by innovative work conditions, which are more flexible and if used correctly and with social responsibility they can help parents in responding to family tasks without inhibiting their professional evolution. However, as mentioned before there have been serious concerns and objections to this issue by feminist institutions and trade unions that regard most of these innovations as a means of reproducing the traditional gender-based occupational segregation.

The second issue is to define what we mean by "good childcare" and how we can ensure it. In many European countries, including Cyprus, grandmothers have played an important role in children's upbringing.

This is getting harder and harder, though, as often the new family resides away from the paternal one. Furthermore, in the next generation the women that will become grandmothers and will not have to work will be the exception, not the rule. Consequently, there has to be a total strategy on behalf of the state that will respond to this need and that will set high standards regarding childcare and serving the working parents. Where the social services are concerned and especially childcare, it is known that the goals of the Barcelona summit are the provision of childcare for 90% of children aged between three and the mandatory school age and for 33% of children aged below three by 2010. It may be that in Cyprus there could be a great scope, apart from the social necessity, for the needs to be explored as well as the possibilities of improving reconciliation policies and for measures to be adopted to this end. The table below shows the rates of meeting childcare needs in the European countries:

Table: Childcare services in the E.U.

State	Rate of coverage for children up to 3 years old	Rate of coverage of children between 3 and the mandatory school age
Belgium	30	97
Denmark	64	91
Germany	10	78
Greece	3	46
Spain	5	84
France	29	99
Ireland	38	56
Italy	6	95
Holland	6	95
Austria	4	68
Poland	12	75
Finland	22	66
Sweden	48	80
U.K.	34	60

Source: OECD data

Thoughts and Notes on the Issues of Reconciliation
of Work and Family Life in Europe.

9

The European Union has illuminated women regarding its policy on equal opportunities of access to the society and employment (Jaurnotte, 2003). Within this frame there have been a number of laws aiming at the harmonisation of personal/family and professional life. It regards provisions that both directly and indirectly help employees and especially women to combine paid labour and family responsibilities. It includes legislation that aims at protecting family and motherhood, legislation that promotes gender equality, legislation regarding provision of care to dependent individuals, legislation about flexibility of time and forms of employment as well as various forms of leave, legislation establishing the grant of various benefits and legislation regarding work hours of the social infrastructure of the state. A wide range of institutional provisions is covered, complemented by the provisions of the collective labour contracts of both the private and the public sector (Mouriki, 2006). It should be noted, however, that the issue of Gender Equality and Equal Opportunities is not an exclusive responsibility of the European Union and its bodies, or the national governments. It constitutes a responsibility of the European society itself, the society of political ideas, social institutions, movements etc[5]. Employing agencies, for example, should realise the negative economic – business implications resulting from the loss of human talents, skills, ideas and innovation because of gender prejudices. The incitement and alertness of the society is, as the E.U. points out, about the need to change behaviour, attitudes, rules and values that define and affect the roles of the sexes in the society, through education, training, the media, arts, culture and science. The elimination of the existing cultural prejudices and social stereotypes is of great importance for the establishment of equality between men and women. The E.U. also points out that the perpetuation of women's negative or stereotypical images, especially in the Media, in electronic communication and entertainment, in advertising and educational material, does not provide a clear and realistic image of the multiple roles of men and women, or their contribution to a changing world. Without interfering with their freedom of expression, the Media and culture industries, as formulators of the public opinion and means of forming values, should contribute to changing stereotypes, public attitude and to presenting a fairer image of men and women.

More specifically, the following have been established at a community level:

-*The Community Charter of Fundamental Social Rights for Workers in 1989.* This Charter makes clear that in order to achieve equality between men and women there should be an intensification of the actions related to equal access to work, payment, terms of employment, education and training.

-*The Charter of Fundamental Rights of the European Union in 2000.* The Charter is a net of protection for the family, but also any individual that wishes to combine family and work without facing the danger of dismissal for reasons related to motherhood. At the same time, they are given the privilege of paid maternity leave and parental leave after birth or adoption.

-*Directive 92/85/EEC* on the introduction of measures to encourage improvements in the safety and health at work of pregnant workers and workers who have recently given birth or are breastfeeding.

-*The Council Recommendation* (92/241/EEC) of 31 March 1992 on childcare.

-*Directive 96/34/EC* of 3 June 1996, on the framework agreement on parental leave concluded by UNICE, CEEP and the ETUC.

-*Directive 93/104/EC,* amended by Directive 2000/34/EC on the organisation of working time that limits maximum weekly working time to 48 hours (1993 and 2000).

-*Directives 2000/43/EC* of 29 June 2000, implementing the principle of equal treatment between persons irrespective of racial or ethnic origin and *2000/78/EC* of 27 November 2000, establishing a general framework for equal treatment in employment and occupation in order to combat discrimination based on religion or belief, disability, age or sexual orientation.

Thoughts and Notes on the Issues of Reconciliation
of Work and Family Life in Europe.

11

-The Resolution of the Council and the Ministers for Employment and Social Policy of 2000 on the balanced participation of men and women in family and working life.

-The Council decision of 20 December 2000, on a programme relating to the community framework strategy on gender equality (2001-2005) (KETHI, 2001).

-The Roadmap for Equality between Men and Women 2006-2010 of the European Commission.

In the Roadmap for Equality, which includes planning for the following five years, the reconciliation of family and professional life is itself one of the main six objectives of the European policy, next to equal economic independence and no longer a means for increasing women's participation in labour.

Apart from the above, already since the 1980s a series of measures aimed at the protection of motherhood and family in general, with emphasis on regulating working time (1981), parental leaves (1989), childcare and the protection of pregnant women (1992) etc. Directive 93/104/EC set the minimum limits for informal employment that regard safety, health, daily and weekly rest etc., whereas already since 1989 the Social Charter acknowledged that parental leave is a major social right of employees and it acquires legal power with a community directive of 1996. According to the E.U., parental leave is distinguished from motherhood leave and is defined as having minimum duration of three months. The manner and details of administration are defined by national laws and collective agreements, while in 2002 both parents are granted the right to parental leaves. The Social Charter places emphasis on the importance of childcare, aiming at the reconciliation of work and family for working parents, while in 1992 the issue of security and health of pregnant workers and workers who have recently given birth or are breastfeeding is introduced.

The European Union in time detected that the current discriminations of structural nature connected to sex, as well as the double and often multiple discrimination experienced by many categories of women (immigrants, heads of single parent families, long time unemployed, etc.) and the wider asymmetry between men and women (Gasouka, 2004) call for the continuation and intensification of community action in the field of Equal Opportunities, as well as the adoption of new methods and approaches to this particular issue. This philosophy is also expressed in the Platform for Action of the Fourth World Conference on Women in Beijing (15/09/1995), according to which one of the strategic objectives of the United Nations is to eliminate discrimination against women and to remove all obstacles towards achieving quality.

Already since 2000 (March 23-24), the Lisbon summit placed special emphasis on the importance of expanding equal opportunities in policies regarding employment, including a decrease in the occupational segregation between men and women and a contribution to the reconciliation of family and professional life. The European Council has taken a step further, by connecting a smooth, free of gender discrimination inclusion of women in the labour market and equal opportunities between the sexes with wider qualitative targets of great importance, such as that of increasing the rate of employed women to 60% by 2010, the main target being the ability of women's full access to a knowledge-based economy, as well as supporting their participation in it, given that information and communication technologies (ICTs) have a growing influence on employment altogether. The role of the Structural Funds – these financial tools of the Community aiming at reinforcing cohesion, improving employment perspectives and promoting sustainable development – in achieving equality between men and women is clearly emphasized. Nowadays their operational regulations take matters of gender equality very seriously during the process of programming, realisation, monitoring and assessment.

However, despite the designing, all measures adopted and generally efforts put in all levels, the fact remains that more than 55 million E.U. citizens are characterised as poor and the vast majority of those are women. Thus there is still the issue of studying the living conditions

Thoughts and Notes on the Issues of Reconciliation
of Work and Family Life in Europe.

13

of these women and the ability of their access to systems of social security (Anker, 1997). At the same time women in the Community still constitute the majority of people employed in "flexible" forms of work, of the unemployed and long-term unemployed. They are still underpaid for work of equal labour quality, time and qualifications; they face the "glass ceiling" phenomenon in their professional evolution and they are under-represented in centres of economic, political and social decision making (Gasouka, 2007). The occupational segregation in male and female professions, women's professional immobility and their limited presence in managerial positions together with an increased participation in informal forms of work are more than clear. It is also known that women comprise the larger percentage of the unemployed and long-term unemployed in the majority of the European countries as well. Men and women employees are still not evenly distributed in professions, sectors and forms of employment. Men usually assume positions of status with higher wages in relation to women (unequal access) who are the first to suffer the consequences of any financial crises (Gasouka, 2007).

Finally, the downward trend of traditionally "female" professions due to the introduction of new technologies renders women's vocational training/re-specialisation immediately indispensable, so that they are in a position to meet the demands of the new work positions (Ellinas & Gasouka, 2007).

The gender-based occupational segregation stems from the socialisation process of the sexes, the restrictions that women face regarding paid labour (gender-based division of household labour or a social state based on the family model of the breadwinner husband and his dependent wife) and from the gender discrimination in the labour market. Thus in the design and realisation of the Framework Strategies (1 & 2) there is an emergence of activities of research, study but practice as well, both at the level of the E.U. and the member states that regarded the analysis of women's position in the labour market, the implementation of equality legislation, the effect and impact of social protection and taxation on men and women, individual access to medical and health care, to the systems of social security and pension, the inherent inability of organisation of labour, etc. in particular, both the E.U. and the national administrations (among those Spain, Greece and Cyprus) take action to the direction of:

> **The reduction of gender-based division of the labour market** by activating education and training (placing emphasis on new technologies), reinforcing positive actions inside businesses by establishing motives and highlighting their social role, encouraging women's employment in traditionally "male" professions and men's employment in care professions, actually promoting equal opportunities in all sectors and levels, enhancing the gender dimension in the relation between school and labour market etc.

> **The reconciliation of family and professional life,** a main E.U. priority already since 2002, as it constitutes a critical factor of European policy regarding employment and the process of social inclusion as it is acknowledged as an exceptionally important factor in the quality of family life and employment.

Especially in the European Roadmap for Equality that succeeded the Framework – Strategy and where a plan for the following five years is developed, the reconciliation of family and professional life is on its own one of the six main goals of the European policy, next to equal economic independence and not any more as a means to increasing women's participation in labour. In this Roadmap the achievement of the Barcelona goals as a key action is complemented and included in the actions that express the commission's will. For this reason the Commission promotes the exchange of good practices between member states and ensures that the structural funds will finance structures and programmes for the promotion of reconciliation. The EQUAL initiatives have particularly promoted clearly innovative ideas in this field.

Thoughts and Notes on the Issues of Reconciliation
of Work and Family Life in Europe.

15

It is evident that since 2001 the reconciliation of family and professional life has been a priority of the European Strategy for Equality. From now on, though, the importance of this goal is upgraded and certain means to its achievement are developed. One of those means is for instance the provision of adequate economic and accessible care services for children, the elderly and the disabled. In this field there is an important contribution of the local government in developing a methodology and planning policy at a local level, a policy that through dissemination in Municipalities and Communities may constitute planning for the entire state (Den & Den, 2001).

1.2. The community framework strategy on gender equality 2001-2005 [1]

In June 2000 the European Commission issued an Announcement to the Council, the European Parliament, the Economic and Social Committee and the Committee of the Regions titled *"Towards a Social Strategy on Gender Equality (2001-2005)"*. This text says that the aim of the Community for that period was the equality between men and women project to take on the form of a coherent strategy, which would include all the community policies in its efforts. This would be done either by adapting these policies proactive intervention or by implementing specific actions aiming at improving the situation of women in the society reactive interventions (Committee of European Communities, 2000). According to the Announcement, this comprehensive strategy marked a significant change in relation to the previous community action on equal opportunities for men and women, which until then was mainly based on departmental activities and on programmes that were funded according to different special budget lines. The framework strategy on equality aimed at the coordination of all the different initiatives and programmes in a common procedure, which would be based on clear evaluation criteria, monitoring tools, setting reference points and gender proofing. So the new approach would raise the level of the broad sphere of existing community activities for the promotion of equality and would secure their comprehensive cohesion. Furthermore, this improved framework strategy was expected to guarantee the better monitoring and distribution of the results of the actions.

In this planning for the previous five years, the Commission set the basic aims, which were separated into five related sectors of intervention. According to the framework strategy, all the community activities related to gender would clearly be linked to one or more of the following sectors: Economic life, equal participation in representation, social rights, everyday life and the roles and stereotypes concerning both genders. The main priority in the aforementioned framework was the promotion of the equality of women in the economic life, through the reduction of the professional differentiation and the work-life balance. Indeed, the Lisbon European Council, as we noted, has set quantitative aims for the equal participation of men and women in the economic life, such as the one concerning the increase of the employment of women percentage from 51% in 2000 to 60% by 2010. We mainly see that the framework strategy on gender equality brought about methodological changes in the until then policy on the issue. It introduced the concept of cohesion of the actions and set the aim of spreading them. The monitoring and evaluation tools are of great importance for the implementation of gender mainstreaming, that is introducing equality in all policies and on all levels. Gender mainstreaming is at this moment the methodological and substantive aim of the policies on equality and is considered to be a big step in the way to abolishing inequalities in all sectors.

In this planning for the following five years, the Commission defined the main objectives, which are distributed in five inter-related fields of action. Based on the framework strategy all the community actions related to gender would be clearly connected to one or more of the following fields: economic life, equal participation and representation, social rights, civil life and gender roles and stereotypes (Gasouka, 2007). A main priority to the above framework was the

Thoughts and Notes on the Issues of Reconciliation
of Work and Family Life in Europe.

17

promotion of women's equality in economic life through a reduction in occupational segregation and the reconciliation of professional and family life. The Council of Europe at Lisbon has set qualitative objectives for equal participation of men and women in economic life, such as the one regarding an increase in the rate of women's employment from 51% in 2000 to 60% by 2010. finally, in the recent Charter for Equality, which includes planning for the following five years, the reconciliation of family and professional life is itself one of the main six objectives of the European policy (Jaurnotte, 2003, Gasouka, 2007, 2008).

Despite, however, the encouraging data that result from gender European policies and strategies of the last decade, it is common ground that there is still a long road ahead to achieving the reconciliation and equal opportunities in general. The lack of a structured political reconciliation is to a large extent due to the impressive lack of demand for policies that are family-friendly, both from the point of view of the trade unions and that of employees. This is not true only in "male-dominated" fields, as someone might expect, but in all fields. As there are no empirical data that interpret this phenomenon, we can only make guesses as to the reasons. The following inhibiting factors are mentioned quite indicatively:

(a) survival of informal support networks
(b) employers' reluctance to provide their employees greater flexibility for their work hours
(c) women's under-representation in trade unions
(d) exceptionally low rate of women in higher and highest ranks of syndicate hierarchy
(e) lack of information regarding the existing family friendly policies implemented in other European countries
(f) fear of income loss
(g) massive resort to overtime employment

From the side of employers' too there are significant obstacles in the implementation and dissemination of initiatives for the reconciliation of family and work:

1. the high cost these policies entail
2. the dominant mentality and attitude of managerial staff
3. the dominance, in the majority of businesses, of Taylor's system of organisation of production and labour, which leaves no space for innovation and flexibility
4. the lack of policies of staff retention.

Apart from some measures of supporting the family beyond the employees' statutory rights, the result of the above is that very few businesses are consistent in adopting policies that promote a balance between professional and non-professional life.

The overall conclusion is therefore that the effort to successfully combine family and professional life meets a number of *obstacles* that create a negative ambience, such as:

(a) certain law provisions, for example the fact that parental leave is unpaid.
(b) the structure of the business sector, with the overwhelming predominance of small and medium businesses.
(c) the predominance of anachronistic methods of organising labour.
(d) the survival of traditional models and attitudes regarding role distribution between the sexes, mainly inside the family.
(e) the lack (or absence) of incorporating the dimension of reconciliation of family/work, both in the agenda of collective negotiations, the business culture and the society in general.
(f) low wages.

Thoughts and Notes on the Issues of Reconciliation
of Work and Family Life in Europe.

19

1.3. *The road map for equality between women and men (2006-2010)*

In the Road Map for Equality (European Commission, 2006), which elaborates on the planning for the next five years, the work-family life balance is by itself one of the six main aims of the European policy, alongside equal financial independence, and not a means to increase the participation of women in work any more. The reconciliation of family and professional life can also be defined as the balance of professional and family obligations. The new term refers to the equal participation of men and women in family responsibilities in a way that allows both genders to meet their professional obligations and to utilize their creativity and skills in the workplace. The shared responsibility of the couple in the workplace - which will contribute to their professional advancement - is a precondition for the implementation of this new policy, which comes to complement and promote the policy of gender mainstreaming. The actions provided for in order to meet this aim are:

1. The flexible regulation of working hours both for women and men. These policies are thought to facilitate the creation of a flexible economy, while improving the living conditions of the citizens. They also help the people to remain in the labour market, utilizing all their potential. However, despite these positive aspects of flexible work, which the Commission text refers to, it is noted that these regulations concern women to a greater degree, thus creating an imbalance between the genders, which has adverse effects on the professional situation of women and their financial independence.

2. The increase and improvement of care services.[6]
Europe has to face a triple challenge concerning the demographic issue. The shrinking of the active population, the reduction in the birthrate and the increase of the population of an older age. The regulations that will lead to a better work-private life balance are part

of the solution of the demographic problem, providing affordable and accessible infrastructure for childcare, as demanded according to the Barcelona aims. As already mentioned, according to these aims, by 2010 appropriate services will cover 90% of children from three years of age until they enter primary education, and at least 33% of children up to three years of age. They also provide for services to meet the needs of caring for elderly persons and persons with disabilities. The quality of these services must be improved and at the same time the qualifications of the respective population, which will be mainly made up of women, must be developed and acknowledged.

3. <u>Improved reconciliation policies for women and men.</u>
The structures and services are adapted to the modern reality, where men and women work, at a very slow rate. However, very few men take parental leave or are part-time employed (7.4% compared to 32.6% of women). So the women hold the main care of the children and other dependant members of the family. The men must be encouraged to undertake more family responsibilities, mainly through the larger utilization of parental and paternal leave.

In the Road Map achieving the Barcelona aims as a key action is completed and is placed among the actions expressing the special will of the Commission. For this reason, the Commission is promoting the exchange of good practices among member states and assures that the structural funds will sponsor structures and programmes for the promotion of reconciliation. The EQUAL initiatives especially promote the innovative ideas in this field.

Since 2001, work-family life balance is a priority of the European Strategy on Equality. From now on, however, the meaning of this aim is upgraded and specific means are set out to meet it. One of these means is the provision of adequate affordable and accessible services for the care of children, elderly persons and persons with disabilities. In this sector the contribution of the local administration is especially important both in developing the methodology and in drafting policy

Thoughts and Notes on the Issues of Reconciliation
of Work and Family Life in Europe.

21

on a local level, a policy which by being spread to the municipalities and the communities can constitute the planning for the whole of the country. Furthermore, the local administration organizations for some years now have the experience of relevant structures, such as child centers, as well as the responsibility to implement programmes such as "Help at Home". Thus, they have the tools to promote the aims set out by the road map on equality by the year 2010.

1.4. Family and gender

The definition of roles that are traditionally attributed to the social categories of gender is the innate result of an economic system and socio-psychological processes that are reinforced in a dialectic manner. The stratification of western society in classes is accompanied by a gender-based social asymmetry. Everywhere the relation between male/female is a relation of hierarchy: hierarchy based on law or custom, where laws and rules come in. This specific hierarchised system, as any other, is surrounded by myths and notions in order to secure its legitimation and acceptance, attributing the fact of gender asymmetry to natural or supernatural factors. At the same time, it develops a set of attitudes and representations, that is a social conscience and a gender-based values scale that entails diverse behaviours and expectations by gender and composes what we have lately got accustomed to calling in the social sciences – thanks to feminist thinking and research – social role of gender (Gasouka, 2004). The traditional gender representations are profoundly integrated in the temper of people who constitute society. This fact does not refer only to men, but also the majority of women that have "internalised" these representations since early childhood – a phenomenon beyond class (Kokkinou, 2008). A first social transfer of gender models is realised within the family, since a child's conception till birth and during the care of the infant, in the way it is brought up and then educated. The formation of gender images and values by which it is shaped begins very early. The parents transfer their gender attitudes through their actions and by setting limitations, shaping the child's behaviour with an entire role-play game, with adult-children exchanges and by reinforcing this attitude using encouragement or punishment. The parents' behaviour is of course a product of their own upbringing, enhanced and corrected by their current social status, by their personal preferences and the value system they have adopted.

It is exactly within the frame of the systems of the representations of western nuclear families, where gender social roles are generally formed and family time between men and women, minors and adults, is distributed. In these processes of regulating family life the women are burdened with multiple roles and responsibilities in relation to men, whereas on the other hand (precisely as a result of these roles) they enter the labour market in harder conditions than their companions. They are often forced to abandon their "vital professional space" and relevant personal needs and expectations (evolution, higher salaries etc.) submitting them to family obligations and the care of the dependent members of the family (children, the elderly etc.). Life, however, and everyday needs require a redefinition of the social roles of the sexes inside the family and provide fatherhood with new content and dynamics[7]. This new dynamic in the relationship between father – child[8], an expanded, practical participation of men in family obligations and their involvement especially with children should constitute the modern social family reality. To this direction, this paternal role[9] needs social acceptance and support, a role that transcends gender stereotypes and prejudices, as it contributes both to the communication and contact between spouses and children's better upbringing (Kokkinou, 2008) .

However, apart from family relations and social roles as they are fulfilled within the family, the contribution to the transcendence of the gender inequalities of the State and its bodies is of decisive importance. A family exists in a certain socio-economic and cultural environment by which it is directly influenced (and influences it by

Thoughts and Notes on the Issues of Reconciliation
of Work and Family Life in Europe.

23

its turn). Consequently, the way that the State supports and reinforces new family relationships, ensuring at the same time women's mild and equivalent entrance to the labour market, is related both to the legislative framework and the existence of the necessary supporting social structures. The protection of motherhood as well as the expansion and upgrade of the paternal role are very important in the specific provision of the State (Den & Den, 2001). At a European level there is an effort to promote various kinds of maternity, paternity and parental leaves, with a simultaneous prevention of unfavourable consequences, whose enactment may entail obstacles for women's access to employment, working conditions and their ability to assume managerial positions. Men are also encouraged to participate in their children's upbringing already since birth or their integration into the family. According to the legislation of the Court of the European Communities, the protection of the mother by the community law aims at the protection "on one hand of the biological condition of the woman during the pregnancy and after that, and on the other hand the special relationship of the woman and her child during the period following pregnancy and equality", but also the "achievement of actual and not formal gender equality". The central community text is Directive 92/85 on the introduction of measures to encourage improvements in the safety and health at work of pregnant workers and workers who have recently given birth or are breastfeeding (Dex, Smith & Winter, 2001).

Distribution table of the rate of employees who believe that their working hours are reconciled very well with their family and social obligations per country.

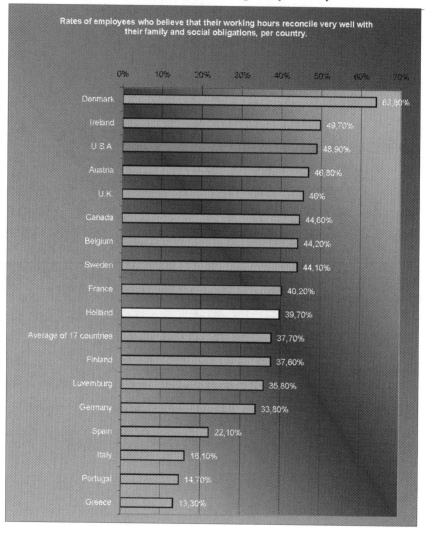

Rates of employees who believe that their working hours reconcile very well with their family and social obligations, per country.

Denmark	63,80%
Ireland	49,70%
U.S.A	48,90%
Austria	46,80%
U.K.	46%
Canada	44,60%
Belgium	44,20%
Sweden	44,10%
France	40,20%
Holland	39,70%
Average of 17 countries	37,70%
Finland	37,60%
Luxemburg	35,80%
Germany	33,80%
Spain	22,10%
Italy	16,10%
Portugal	14,70%
Greece	13,30%

Thoughts and Notes on the Issues of Reconciliation
of Work and Family Life in Europe.

25

Table: Rate of employees who believe their working hours are "very well"
combined with their family and social obligations.

Rate of employees who believe their working hours are "very well" combined with their family and social obligations								
		State of employment		Sex		Age		
	Total of employee	Self-employed	Employees	Men	Women	< 25 years old	25-44 years old	45-64 years old
Denmark	63.8	61.0	63.9	62.7	65.0	56.4	59.0	74.4
Ireland	49.7	33.3	53.7	44.2	58.3	53.2	47.2	51.7
U.S.A.	48.9	50.9	48.4	44.7	53.4	43.7	44.0	55.4
Austria	46.8	38.7	47.9	44.8	49.4	46.9	46.5	47.7
Un. Kingdom	45.5	42.6	46.2	37.8	54.9	47.5	44.1	45.7
Canada	44.6	47.0	44.0	41.8	47.6	37.4	41.3	51.1
Belgium	44.2	31.9	46.7	43.3	45.6	44.5	42.6	47.8
Sweden	44.1	48.5	43.8	43.3	45.1	35.2	41.4	49.6
France	40.2	32.7	41.4	38.8	41.9	43.5	36.9	44.9
Holland	39.7	48.0	39.1	36.2	44.6	39.5	37.4	44.2
Finland	37.6	26.2	39.5	35.6	40.0	34.5	36.6	39.7
Luxembourg	35.8	41.4	35.2	34.8	37.5	43.1	32.2	43.2
Germany	33.8	30.4	33.8	29.8	39.3	36.0	30.8	37.1
Spain	22.1	20.7	22.5	19.6	26.8	26.6	20.1	24.0
Italy	16.1	14.6	16.5	15.3	17.4	23.9	13.5	16.8
Portugal	14.7	18.1	13.5	15.1	14.3	12.0	14.6	15.9
Greece	13.3	6.9	18.3	11.9	15.6	14.1	14.2	12.2
Average of 17 countries	*37.7*	*34.9*	*38.5*	*35.3*	*41.0*	*37.5*	*35.4*	*41.3*

Source: OECD Labour Market Statistics — Indicators; 2001 data except for Germany
and the U.K. that are 2000 data.

Regarding childcare and other dependent members of the family, the existing research, as well as overall experience from Cyprus, demonstrates that women have the principal household care. The Roadmap for Equality mentions that in average European women dedicate at least 4 hours daily on household tasks, whereas men a little over than 2 hours. It is logical to assume that in Cyprus, where the traditional stereotypes for the roles of men and women at work and the home are still powerful, this gap is bigger. More specifically, a publication of the European Foundation for the Improvement of Living and Working Conditions entitled "Fertility and Family Issues in an Enlarged Europe" (2004) presents comparative rates about the European countries regarding the following: a) how many European citizens believe that they are content with the number of children they have – it appears that there is a majority of people who say they are content with the number of children they have. b) On the other hand, there is quite a large number (about one third of those asked) who state that they would like more children if the economic and social conditions of their lives would permit so. Finally there is a smaller rate of 10% to 15% who support that they have more children than they wished. From the above data we can conclude the following: a) that the discrepancies between actual and ideal family size tend to expand to both directions and b) that external factors limit an important part of the population from further childbearing.

The unit of the research of the European Foundation for the Improvement of Living and Working Conditions entitled "Fertility and Family Issues in an Enlarged Europe" presents the following data: the belief that childcare should be given by both parents characterises a percentage of 81,8% of the citizens in Europe of the 15 member states, and 80% in Europe of 25. Among these countries Greece has one of the middle positions. However, in the qualitative characteristics of the study we see that the specific activities that fathers are thought they should take on are sports, help with the homework, responsibility for punishment, answering important questions of the children etc. On the contrary, the rates of citizens that maintain that care such as dressing, changing

Thoughts and Notes on the Issues of Reconciliation
of Work and Family Life in Europe.

27

and tucking children in bed are both parents' responsibility, are very lower. This information is an indication that mothers are burdened with more everyday care, the one that cannot be put off because it serves basic children's needs, but also the one that is characterised as the less creative and pleasant. It is precisely that kind of activity that may deter women from seeking and keeping a work position with possibilities of evolution. From that research we get information that may be useful in understanding men and women's needs, aiming at the reconciliation of family and professional life. The father's participation is vital in children's upbringing (O'Brien & Shelmit, 2003). A good practice implemented by some European States is the paternity leave. In Scandinavian countries the paternity leave ranges from 10 to 20 days. The term "paternity leave" included in Directive 2002/73 refers to *"the balanced participation of women and men in family and working life, prohibits any relevant forms of discrimination and grants working men an individual and untransferable right to paternity or adoption leave, while maintaining their rights relating to employment.* It can be granted together with the maternity leave regardless of the duration of the maternity and paternity leaves and has been successfully established as paid leave in several European countries (National Commission for Human Rights, 2006).

Another piece of information that may be of use from the same issue has to do with the politics that are deemed by the citizens themselves to be the most important and helpful for parents and future parents. Greek men and women, for example, consider childcare services rather low in their priorities, on the contrary, policies regarding combating unemployment, tax reductions and child benefits are in the top three positions. Three assumptions can be made:

a) high levels of unemployment, long working hours and low wages that impose a rather low standard of living on Greek people render the safeguard of decent employment more imperative and a precondition for an increase in birth rates.

b) The contribution of the elder generation, low rates of female employment and the possibility of cheap, uninsured female employment, mostly economic immigrants for child keeping, does not allow the need for organised care services to show its real extent.

c) In Greece the traditional mentality, which is still quite powerful, requires that a "good" mother prioritise children's upbringing by interrupting or delaying her professional participation and evolution.

Assigning, therefore, care to organised services may be considered as a necessity solution that does not lead to correct children's upbringing. It is obvious that on a second level and aiming at long-term results it will take overall changes both to the way of organising labour and to the mentality of Greek citizens, men and women, those that are now young adults and the children that will be the future citizens and parents. It should be interesting to see the latest data, in which Cyprus is included, and to examine how contradictions are solved such as the one between low levels of female unemployment and social attitudes and mentalities that are common with Greece.

1.5. The gender dimension in businesses

In the public and private sector businesses, women workers are facing a series of difficulties and obstacles reflecting the broader social prejudices linked to the genders. One matter concerns the working conditions: timetables, difficulties in accessing adequate parental leave and restricted access to childcare services, consulting services etc in the framework of large enterprises (Dex, Smith & Winter, 2001). Another problem is the inadequate information of women regarding their rights in family-friendly policies (often even of men).The second matter has to do with the discrimination against women during recruitment and their professional advancement. The unemployment of women - which in Greece especially, in contrast to Cyprus, is double that of men - and

Thoughts and Notes on the Issues of Reconciliation
of Work and Family Life in Europe.

29

the phenomenon of the "glass roof / glass wall", make the position of women in work more difficult and reproduce and/or broaden gender inequalities. It is worth mentioning in brief some terms and conditions concerning inter-business life and communication, in order to better comprehend the meaning of adopting equality strategies in businesses. More specifically:

The term "glass ceiling" (Liapi & Tzavara, 2005) was adopted in 1986 by "Wall Street Journal" journalists with an aim to describe the artificial or invisible barriers (based on views and prejudices) that slow down or block the professional advancement of women in higher and senior hierarchy positions in businesses, and was later broadened in the sense of a wall, in order to describe the invisible but omnipresent exclusion of women from prestigious jobs. Both the horizontal and vertical division is linked to the stereotypes regarding genders and the discrimination women are faced with in other sectors of their lives. A characteristic of the horizontal division in the professional place is that women are gathered in sectors identified with stereotype feminine roles in the family, while one of the causes of the vertical division is the notion that the main "work" of women is the care of the household and the family and thus a career and paid work are complementary (Gasouka, 2007).

We can mention in a few words that the position of women in businesses through the four theoretical issues, as mentioned in the publication of K.E.TH.I. *"In order", theories for organisation and gender* (Wahl, Hook, Holgersson, & Linghag, 2005). The first is *structure*. That is the way in which work is allocated in businesses, services and departments, as well as the way in which these are structured vertically and horizontally. In relation to the genders, the questions raised are the following: What is the distribution of men and women in numbers, if there is a marginalization of the genders regarding the objectives, the specialisation and the positions men and women take over, the form of the gender hierarchical distribution, the breadth of influence and authority of men and women etc.When we speak of structure in businesses we are referring to:

- The **structure of opportunities** that is the possibility of moving and advancing within the business.
- The **structure of authority** that is the possibility of effective activity within the business.
- The **composition of the groups**, in minority and majority, meaning the ration of men and women in working groups and departments.

The structures determine the way in which the persons function, if they have high or low confidence, if they take initiatives in the end, and if they are creative in their workplace, if they offer all that they can.

The second theoretical matter is *leadership*. How businesses are managed is a central question to the theory of organizations and has been approached by different angles (Collins,2001). The study of leadership issues from the gender point of view can be categorized based on three main questions: How are the women bosses? Why are there so few women in senior positions? In which way is leadership gender defined? An to this a fourth question can be added: How does leadership change? These questions cannot be elaborated on here. It is however necessary to note that, according to studies, homogeneity and conformism are strong phenomena in the ranks of the directors (Wahl , Hook , Holgersson, & Linghag, 2005). This results in the ranks of directors to reproduce themselves and their characteristics. Thus women reaching high positions in the hierarchy, burdened with uncertainty and competition, fully adopt the characteristics of a group that is traditionally held by men. The demands from managing officers according to the traditional distribution of work, where the director is a man and, if he has a family, its responsibility lies with the wife, are increased in time and dedication (Den & Den, 2001). So these issues

Thoughts and Notes on the Issues of Reconciliation
of Work and Family Life in Europe.

31

have to be discussed in the framework of the businesses in order to promote changes in the direction of equal participation of women with respect to family life.

The third issue is *symbolism* and its contribution to the structure of the inter-business world and its reconstructions. The debate around symbolism in businesses begins from the position that the organizations in general are considered to be cultural expressions from the gender aspect. It concerns the symbols linked to gender and the gender state of order in businesses. The businesses are man-held organizations with respective cultures. The female directors, for example, have been described as *"travelers in a world of men"*, aiming at determining the businesses as cultures foreign to women. The jobs are determined according to gender, leading to marginalization. In this context, the women in businesses are listed as members of a suppressed minority.

Respectively, the Discourse uttered and developed in businesses is characterized as a Discourse of dominance and suppression. With the term "Discourse" a whole system of ways of thought is described, which seals the views, the language and the practice of people. When the concept "Discourse" is used, it is always attributed to a central meaning in language, which is a central factor for understanding a gender state of order as something symbolic and the understanding of people as cultural beings. If we do not comprehend the above, it is not possible to form a public debate that will break through prejudice and create a new balance in businesses and in the family life with equal treatment and participation.

There is resistance and obstacles to this change, which are based on the aforementioned theoretical issues. The structures characterizing the public and private life are based on the reactions of men and women, who often feel more comfortable in the older situation, even if it appears to be unfair and dysfunctional. The planning and implementation of equality schemes in businesses is an action necessary for the effectiveness of every action on a social level. For the planning and implementation of long-term aims, which in the end are the comprehensive political intervention for equality, the improvement of living conditions and the creative participation in work and family, procedures to cultivate the awareness of the population are necessary in all grades of education from a gender aspect (Bond, Hyman & Wise, 2002). Also necessary is an intervention in the way the gender stereotypes in work and the family are presented by the mass media and advertisements, and finally publicizing and promoting actions on equality carried out by the organizations on all levels.

Apart from the aforementioned, gender research reaffirms that, in microeconomic level, staff policies that incorporate the gender equality dimension are beneficial not only for employees but also employers, since they contribute to a reduction in absences and growth in business productivity/competitiveness as well as the wider local and regional development in general.

It is not certain that the majority of businesses have left behind the stereotypes regarding the role and usefulness of female employment. The tendency of some businesses, mostly small and medium ones, to reproduce obsolete attitudes and practices, that maintain labour inequality between the sexes, undermines a couple's smooth family life. In several cases, the unequal treatment of a couple by businesses on matters of professional evolution, wages, assignment of managerial positions may even cause trouble in their private-personal lives, especially when the spouses are of equal educational-professional background.

By attributing too much of importance to cases like for example the "cost of absence" of a working mother (maternity leaves, parental benefits etc.), business often fail to understand the multiple benefit that equal treatment entails for themselves. All research points to the fact that provision of equal work opportunities to men and women contributes to growth in business productivity and competitiveness (Gasouka, 2007). Policies of attracting better human resources, regardless of sex, may offer knowledge, skills, innovation and quality services to the business. All that evidence cover whatever women's "absence cost" and help the

Thoughts and Notes on the Issues of Reconciliation
of Work and Family Life in Europe.

33

business gradually acquire high level specialised labour resource, which is a precondition for its development and evolution in the contemporary competitive economic environment (European Commission, 2006). Another issue that highlights the influence of businesses on a couple's family-professional life is related to the family changes brought by the simultaneous employment of both spouses/parents (Warin, Solomon, Lewis, & Langford, 1999). The gradual increase in women's employability in private and public businesses not only cancels the traditional model of wife/mother that is exclusively involved in the household duties and the children's upbringing, but also introduces new parameters regarding both the internal function of the family and the work place. As a result, the time a working mother dedicates to the household and the children is limited (Jaurnotte, 2003). The amount of time a man should dedicate in the family affairs is raised correspondingly. Quite often help is hired for the household, a fact that burdens the family budget significantly and a phenomenon that is widespread in the Republic of Cyprus. Certain large businesses acknowledge the objective problems of time and expenses faced by the couples that work in them and affect their productivity negatively and promote measures in order to deal with them[10]. Some include the establishment of day care centres at the work place, the elasticity in working hours to mothers that ask for it, the grant of summer leave during school holidays, the implementation of innovative projects for a better organisation of the working time so as to facilitate couples with their family obligations (European Commission, Directorate-General for Employment, Social Affairs and Equal Opportunities, 2006). With these actions they contribute to the harmonisation of the couple's family and professional life and develop a functional relationship of trust and understanding with the corporate staff. It is certain that similar initiatives on the employers' part have a beneficial effect on the workers' performance and raise the business's production and work circle[11]. Additionally, employing organisations in cooperation with the workers' organisations, engage in examining the implementation of new, pilot forms of labour organisation in large and medium businesses. Their principal aim is the reconciliation of family and professional life combined with a reinforcement of women's employment and adaptability, by facilitating their participation in life long learning programmes. To this end they consider practices of flexible use of the possibilities provided by the Information and Communication Technologies (ICTs), the implementation of telework projects, the optional implementation of part-time employment etc. In order for these practices to be successful, they are designed according to the organisational needs of the business and the workers' family/ personal needs[12].

In several west European countries the private and public businesses have started to implement pilot programmes that facilitate the reconciliation of the workers' family and professional life. This harmonisation is expected to be achieved through actions of continuing support to workers with family obligations, as well as with the redefinition of traditional models regarding sex roles. In Austria, for instance, there is a project called "Management of Equality-Quality", which is addressed to business administrations and employing organisations. The aim of the project is the promotion of sensitising companies and employing institutions in matters of equality and the development of measures and organisational structures for the harmonisation of family and professional life for men and women. On the other hand, several European countries place emphasis on the cooperation of the private and the public sector in dealing with the problems that threaten the smooth connection between employees' family and professional life. Thus they examine the possibility that the State grant public and private businesses with economic incentives (e.g. tax reductions) in order to promote, through targeted actions, gender equality at the work place, women's equal participation in programmes of vocational training, but also the constitution of organisational structures to the same businesses that will facilitate working couples.

Several businesses have come to realise that quality human capital can be an asset in modern market economy. It can also function as an

Thoughts and Notes on the Issues of Reconciliation
of Work and Family Life in Europe.

35

important profit multiplier for a business, when it fulfils the necessary conditions and has the knowledge and skills to provide high level services. It is obvious that workers that have a normal family life and balance between home and work without particular problems are more productive and increase the competitiveness of the business. For this reason, medium and large businesses are invited to design and implement actions that aim at exploiting resources in relation to the harmonisation of workers', men and women's family and professional life.

A central role in this effort is played by the employees' familiarisation with Information and Communication Technologies (ICTs), life long learning and ongoing vocational training of the resources of every business. The human capital and the investment in the development of personal skills, in knowledge, in skills as inextricable elements of labour are the driving force for the development and productivity of an enterprise. The introduction and optimisation of ICTs in businesses are expected to lead to a quality upgrade of human resources and to reinforce businesses' competitiveness and profits decisively (Eurobarometer Survey, 2005). The familiarisation of both sexes' employees with the use of the Internet and the development of e-business systems facilitate business activities. It is also important that ICTs can help employees organise their working time to the benefit of their family/personal lives. The widespread use of the Internet, telework, the introduction of flexible work schedules that will facilitate couples working in businesses and distance work can be utilised in order a) to offer businesses quality labour product and b) to facilitate dual career couples in harmonising their private and professional lives.

Furthermore, in cooperation with universities or private educational institutions, businesses can implement injob training programmes for the continuing vocational training of their staff (European Council, 2003). The upgrading of human resources' skills and the investment in knowledge and skills reinforce the productivity of the businesses and shield it against competition. At the same time, there is an upgrade in the role of the employee, who obtains the ability to manage information and new technologies correctly in an ongoing learning process that is continuously renewed.

In this direction, the businesses can play an important role with schemes to utilize all the employees by forming a working environment that is women- and family-friendly and establishing the innovative institution of Equality Advisers within them.

> **Utilization of lifelong learning and providing opportunities for vocational training and organised work experience** with emphasis on women who remain financially inactive, in order to substantively improve their potential to enter/re-enter the labour market.

> **Promotion of modern and flexible forms of employment** for those women who wish to take on such work.

Finally, it is worth making some observations directly linked to the generalised effort to overcome gender discrimination in the private and public sphere of life. More specifically:

Women, despite their social and financial achievements, are still under-represented in political, social and financial decision-making centres. They are the restricted minority in a significant number of European Union countries, in parliaments, government positions, senior trade union bodies, as well as business management, while over 80% of parliamentary deputies worldwide are men. The stereotypes and prejudices identifying the public sphere of life with men and the private life with women, as well as the multiple roles of women, phenomena such as the "glass ceiling", discourage women from seeking authority and responsible positions, and even becoming actively involved in the political and trade union life.

The absence of women from the decision-making centres means that men will continue to set the priorities for the distribution and utilization of resources, social welfare, education, the economy, and women's skills, needs and wishes will remain in the margin. This means a great loss of human resources and talents for the growth effort of EU member states

Thoughts and Notes on the Issues of Reconciliation
of Work and Family Life in Europe.

37

to say the least, by possibly obstructing the full satisfaction of benefits and needs of its people.

The proof of the gender marginalization and the increase of women's participation in political, financial etc decision-making centres is not obviously a matter of increasing numbers but improves and broadens democracy with positive effects on all the citizens (Kokkinou, 2008).

It has been determined that the balanced representation of both genders in decision-making centres leads to the introduction of forgotten and/or new issues in the political, economic, educational, trade union agenda. Experience shows that the involvement of both genders leads to drafting policies that are more harmonized with a civil society in which diversity exists. Furthermore, especially the under-representation of women in political decision-making raises the issue of the legitimacy of existing political structures. When the participation of women in decision-making is extremely restricted or almost inexistent, the legitimacy of political decisions may not be interpreted on the same terms for men and women. This fact could create a general feeling of distrust towards the representative system, resulting in the refusal of women to accept laws and policies that have been passed without their own participation.

The European Commission has intensified over the past few years its recommendations to the national governments to proceed to record the various consequences of the voting systems in the political representation of women in several bodies. Also they should examine the possibility of adapting and/or reforming these systems, and take, if deemed necessary, respective legislative measures and/or encourage the introduction of "quotas" and other measures that promote balanced representation. It also involves establishing measures that could facilitate the exodus of women into the public sphere of life and seeking their participation in decision-making centers, such as inter alias high quality and low cost childcare services, flexible timetables etc. At the same time, the EU proposes the organizing of public opinion awareness campaigns aiming at promoting women's participation in politics and urging the electorate to vote for women, with the active participation of feminist and other women's organizations, NGOs, workers and mass media etc in the effort. On the other hand National and European Programmes of Social Policy, which include measures for achieving equality, offer businessmen the ability to implement *a future management*, that is to be able to predict a desirable future for their business and at the same time to form the conditions that will allow this prediction to become true. Consequently, policies of harmonising workers' family and professional life do not constitute – or should not constitute – a solution for funding businesses by the European Commission, but aim at the development of social awareness and economy.

1.6. *Indicative positive measures and practices of European countries concerning the combination of family and professional life*

The term "positive practices" means *measures, actions and regulations aiming at the facilitation of the combination of family and professional life for men and women* (KETHI, 2006). They are achieved through statutory and general implementation initiatives, through initiatives of the businesses themselves, as well as a product of social consultation among the social partners at sectoral or national level. The good practices of the European Countries are divided in (a) Institutional Initiatives, (2) Business Initiatives and (3) Social Partners' Initiatives (Mouriki, 2006).

Institutional Initiatives • Subsidized care of children of preschool age (e.g. economic benefits to parents taking care of their children themselves, personal coupon for the selection of the kind of childcare, child benefit) • Parents with children under the age of 6 have the right to ask their employers to work under a flexible form of employment in Britain. • Establishment of a universal child's benefit for three years for all parents regardless of their professional status in Austria. • Parents of young children have the ability to get part-time employment fully protected from dismissal and the right to return to full-time employment

Thoughts and Notes on the Issues of Reconciliation
of Work and Family Life in Europe.

39

in Austria. • In the non-profit sector of the economy, establishment of the ability for employees to follow a flexible career, making use of long-term leaves, or combining part-time employment with part-time retirement in Belgium. • Establishment of a 35-hour week, without salary reduction and restriction of overtime employment in France. • State contribution to childcare expenses (covering from 1/3 to 2/3 of the total expense) through tax rebate and the employer's voluntary aid in Holland. • Establishment of the long-term "leave for personal reasons" for employees who are willing to exchange the income from their work with a temporary interruption due to reasons of family care, education, personal development, early retirement etc. in Holland. • Creation of a fund financing measures in the Medium and Small Businesses for the promotion of the reconciliation of family and work, in order to encourage working parents to make use of parental leave and later help them return to their work in Italy. • Creation of institutionally established "Time Offices" functioning under the auspices of municipal authorities in order to encourage and disseminate successful policies and practices of time management developed in other regions in Italy etc.

Business Initiatives • Flexible planning of the labour process and subject, stress management, provision of economic and practical benefits concerning childcare and everyday household needs, staff development, women's re-entrance to work after a long-term absence, sports activities etc. in Finland. • Detection and implementation of employment models that promote gender equality and the reconciliation of family and work, offering women workers the ability to return to work when their children are 2 ½ years old, gives the right to full-time women employees to temporarily ask for part-time employment, imposes the prohibition of mothers' employment at antisocial hours and days at callcenters, while it reorganizes the shift system so that employees can organize their personal life in a much better way in Italy. • Provision of extra benefits to business employees who wish to quit their jobs in order to take care of their children while in the public sector employees who make use of their parental leaves receive 90% of their salary no matter how big it is in Sweden etc.

Social Partners' Initiatives • Personal working time "accounts" are implemented in a chain of businesses as a result of collective agreements in Denmark, Germany, Belgium, France, Sweden. • A collective agreement in the technology sector signed in 2001 anticipates new regulations for the flexibility of working time in Austria. • The Workers' Confederation and the Employers' Union signed a "Memorandum of Understanding" in 2003 in Italy. • A campaign bearing pressure to the government for the establishment of incentives for businesses in order to create a friendlier environment for their employees and introduce regulations for the protection of flexible employment in Britain (KETHI, 2006).

On the other hand, collective bargaining is a very significant institution for the regulation of work relations in all the countries of the European Union. In some of the countries, such as Denmark, Finland and Sweden, very few issues can be regulated by law, since collective bargaining is the primary source of labour law. On the contrary, in countries such as Greece, Spain and Portugal, legislation regulates all terms of employment and defines the rights that can be improved through collective bargaining (KETHI, 2001). In total, however, the European Committee recognises the part of the collective labour agreements for the promotion of both equal opportunities in employment (E.C., COM(2003), 98 final) and the reconciliation of family and professional life for all employees (European Foundation for the Improvement in Living and Working Conditions, 2006). The approach of Collective Negotiations requires attention, as the differentiations in the legal framework, the financial situation, the work relations and the social and family values of each country make their comparison extremely difficult. However, we can recognise a series of positive practices recently implemented through collective labour agreements in several E.U. countries, which could be a useful guide

Thoughts and Notes on the Issues of Reconciliation
of Work and Family Life in Europe.

41

for future collective negotiations in Cyprus. Studying the analysis conducted by the European Foundation for the Improvement in Living and Working Conditions (2006) concerning family-friendly policies included in the latest collective labour agreements in the countries of the E.U. we can distinguish the following positive practices:

i. Belgium: The intersectoral collective agreement of 2001-2, in which the collective negotiations eventuated, provided employees with the right of 1 year-long time credit, the right to have a rest from work equal to 1/5 of the week for 5 years, the right to work 50% or 80% of the full-time shift for employees over 50 years old, the right to special leaves (parental or patient care), with a simultaneous increase of the paternal leave from 3 to 10 days. The most important of all is the new system of time credit, which allows flexible entrance and exit from work both for men and women, in order for them to achieve a reconciliation of professional career and family obligations. The same agreement reduced the maximum of working hours per week from 39 to 38 hours from 2003 without any salary reduction. At the same time, more specific collective agreements, such as that of the mining sector, include even more favourable regulations.

ii. Denmark: Collective agreements have kept the reconciliation of professional and family life high on their priority list for many years. Thus, flexible types of employment are constantly promoted, such as telework, which becomes more and more attractive after the 2000 agreement. Moreover, in 2003 in the collective agreements of certain sectors (economy, production) employees are free to choose individually which part of their income they wish to use for a longer interruption from work, higher salary or pension. In this way they can choose more rest time instead of money. Finally, the flexibility of working time has been promoted by many collective agreements, since a 37-hour week can often be estimated in a much broader period of reference, allowing for working time differentiations from week to week.

iii. Finland: Since 2003 there has been a big effort to reconcile family and professional life through more flexible working hours. Thus, the implementation of a bank of work hours – wherever it is possible – is promoted through sectoral collective agreements.

iv. France: In France in 2004 a national intersectoral agreement was signed concerning gender equality and balanced gender participation in the labour resource and setting the framework for further commitments at sectoral and business level. So, the agreement indicatively (i.e. Renault) provides an increase of part-time employment to those who prefer it, paid maternity leave, reduction of working hours during pregnancy, a two-week extension of the maternity or adoption leave without salary retention, leave of absence for the completion of the adoption procedure, and increased adoption bonus of 1,500€ and extra leave for the care of sick children, while at the same time absences related to maternity, paternity and adoption are included in the real working hours for the calculation of day offs and bonuses.

v. Germany: A collective agreement signed in 2001 promotes equal opportunities in the private sector and the reconciliation of family and professional life for all business employees. Indicatively, women's access to managerial positions is reinforced through the admittance of a larger number of women in relevant training programs and the possibility of part-time employment in those positions.

vi. Italy: In 2003 an innovative local collective agreement was signed in Milan, encouraging parents to use their parental leaves and ensuring retraining programs for them in order to facilitate their smooth reentrance after their leave. In addition, those programs were set to take place during the working hours and even by distance if possible.

Beyond institutional regulations, social partners' organisations have undertaken a series of common initiatives either at sectoral, national or super-national level, in order to facilitate directly or indirectly

Thoughts and Notes on the Issues of Reconciliation
of Work and Family Life in Europe.

43

the reconciliation of family and work. The following are indicative examples:

- In Ireland social partners jointly agreed for a three-year-long "Prosperity and Justice Program" (2000-2003) which covers, among others, several issues concerning the reconciliation of family and work.
- In Britain a joint committee consisting of 22 members "Employers pro balancing work and life" was formed, in order to promote flexible forms of employment.
- Information campaigns take place in several E.U. countries in order to sensitize businesses and public in issues of reconciliation of family and work.
- Personal working time "accounts" are implemented in a number of businesses, as a result of collective agreements (Denmark, Germany, Belgium, Sweden).
- The Belgian National Collective Agreement 2001-2, introduces, among others, innovative measures such as the "Time Credit Program".
- Flexible working hours have been established through numerous sectoral or business agreements, while the same happened lately with telework (i.e. in Italian commerce, German and Italian telecommunications, Danish civil services etc.).

At an E.U. level the inter-occupational organizations of the social partners UNICE, CEEP and CES have so far entered the following framework-agreements (which led the E.U. to issue certain relevant directives and acquired legal status): for the health and safety of pregnant and breast-feeding women (1992), for parental leaves (1995), for part-time employment (1997) and for fixed-term labor agreements (1999). At the same time, the sectoral social dialogue at E.U. level resulted in three agreements regarding the reduction of working time, in the agricultural sector (1997), the railway (1998) and sea transport (1998). Recently, an agreement for the implementation of telework on telecommunications and commerce has been achieved.

Concluding with the positive Reconciliation practices we should point out something: Investigating the legislation of the European countries it is evident that in the framework of the implementation of reconciliation of family and professional life policies, the member-states of the E.U. proceed to the adoption of laws concerning new forms of employment (flexible working hours, personal working time, annual working time management, reduced working time, telework), economic benefits, either direct in the form of salary increase, or indirect in the form of tax-reduction and, finally, the provision of extra leaves for the employees with families ("parental leaves" according to which the parents have to decide who will make use of the leave). In some countries (Norway, Sweden, Iceland) the measure starts to be implemented exclusively for men, especially on the basis "use it or lose it".

Based on the European policy and legislation, the legal rules of the member-states keep expanding and improving in recent years. Here are some indicative legislative regulations applied in Italy, concerning the reconciliation of family and professional obligations: Law 53/2000 on "Provisions for the protection of maternity and paternity, for the right in care and training and for the co-ordination of the working hours in the cities" and the framework-agreement for the experimental implementation of telework in public administration. The regulations including the following issues are common ground for all the member-states:

> Maternity leave: concerns type of leave taken after childbirth, whose duration and compensation level differs from country to country.

> Parental leave: the occasion, duration and payment vary in this type of leave, as well as the policies of its adoption, since some countries have established certain extra incentives for its use by both parents.

Thoughts and Notes on the Issues of Reconciliation
of Work and Family Life in Europe.

45

➤ Adoption leave
➤ Emergency leave
➤ Educational leave
➤ Subsidized care of pre-school aged children: its implementation varies as well, from traditional to very innovative forms, such as economic benefits to parents taking care of their children themselves.

Apart from the common legislation found in all countries, some European countries have proceeded to more specific regulations, which could favour the objective of reconciliation of family and professional life. For instance:

➤ Favorable regulation of parental leaves. In Italy the father deserves extra leave time if he exclusively makes use of it, while in other countries there is the right to share the leave between the two parents
➤ Implementation of telework: in Italy and other countries as well, telework is experimentally implemented 2 to 3 times per week.
➤ Implementation of flexible forms of employment.
➤ Flexible working time arrangement: Since 2000 in Holland a law has been put into effect giving employees the right to increase or reduce their working hours according to their availability.
➤ Increase of the care provision structures through the creation of day nurseries in or near businesses.
➤ Provision of advice and support on issues concerning children's health and care or other personal problems of the employees.
➤ Leaves of absence beyond what has been provided.

At the same time, the following are positive practices at European level: • the creation of an observatory in Italy for flexibility of labour, which observes the consequences of the flexibility measures from the gender perspective • the provision of training opportunities for employees who made use of long-term leaves of absence in Spain, in order to facilitate their return to the labour market • the organisation of training programs in Spain concerning equal opportunities and the sensitisation for those taking part in collective negotiations by the labour organisations of both employees and employers • the "Time credit programme" in Belgium, established by the National Collective Agreement 2001-2002 • the Equality Organisations in Denmark and Sweden, which deserve to defend in court the employees' right to combine their family and professional life in case it has been violated • law regulations for the prohibition of dismissal of female workers who exercise their right to interrupt work for breast-feeding in Spain and Portugal • the legalisation of equality organisations for the initiation of the legal procedure on behalf of the gender based discrimination victims in Denmark and Sweden • the expansion of free legal help before and during legal procedures to all citizens with low salaries and creation of free legal counselling services for everyone in Spain • the legal protection of irregular forms of employment with the safeguarding of protection equivalent to that of the conventional ones etc. Finally, a number of businesses based in Europe, familiar with the European development policy and aiming at keeping their valuable high-rank employees who might quit their jobs because of family obligations, adopt family-friendly practices, such as the creation of day nurseries in their facilities, flexible forms of employment, flexible working hours, extra leaves of absence, etc. (KETHI, 2001 & 2006).

1.7. Afterwards

The entry of women into the labour market, the increase of the female labour force and the improvement of the position of many women in the professional hierarchy in the last years constitute factors that steadily undermine the gender distribution of roles and its traditional interdependences. Indubitably, the involvement of women in the modern economic production with the paid professional employment

Thoughts and Notes on the Issues of Reconciliation
of Work and Family Life in Europe.

47

upsets the fine established balance between the private – female space and the public – male one. Today equality between men and women in all policies constitutes an integral part of the social policy of the European Union and is recognized as a critical factor to its social cohesion and its growth, according to the findings of the European Foundation for the Improvement of Living and Working Conditions, "Quality of Life in Europe" survey (2003). At the centre of interest of the European equality policies lies in the last years is the Reconciliation of Work and Family Life. The need for harmonizing professional and non-professional life (family and household tasks) has gradually gained importance in the last 20 years, because of the increased female participation in employment in all European countries (63% of the women in the E.U. is part of the labour resource), but also of the drastic changes in family models, changes that have led to the increased number of nuclear and single-parent families. The combination of work and family life is a fundamental component of gender mainstreaming in the European strategy for employment and the procedure for social integration. It aims at promoting a more coherent society through the safeguarding of more favorable conditions regarding integration, re-integration and keeping mainly women in the labor market. At the same time it is linked to the development of human resources, business profit, as well as the economic evolution, social cohesion and Democracy. Especially in relation to the world of employers, it has already been made understood that work - life balance contributes to the decrease of differences that are connected to genders and to the improvement of quality in the working environment By the term Reconciliation of Work and Family Life we mean the balanced participation of women and men in the responsibilities and obligations that arise from living together and the common decision to create a family. Reconciliation obviously concerns for both genders – with ulterior purpose the equal sharing of responsibilities – the reformation of the traditional stereotypes regarding the roles of the two genders within and outside the family as well as to guarantee equal opportunities in the procedures of being integrated and remain in employment. In today's reality businesses are called upon to respond to the challenges and requirements of a rapidly changing worldwide socio-economic environment.

In the recent years businesses started to understand the significance of linking the various phases of everyday life for all their staff. The combination of family and professional responsibilities significantly affects the performance of their human resources and finally fixes the highest level of competitiveness – profitability of the business. Besides the national and European social policy programmes that include the measures for the achievement of equality offer the possibility to the entrepreneurs to implement a "foreseeable administration", that is to be able to foresee a desirable future for their business linked to the utilization of both genders in this framework and at the same time to form those conditions that will allow them to make this aspiration come true. As such, the policies to bring the work of the employees in line with the family life do not constitute – or do not have to constitute as it often happens – a solution for subsidizing the businesses on behalf of the European Commission, but they target the development of corporate social responsibility and the economy that they combine them at the same time with the social cohesion but also democracy (Kokkinou, 2008).

NOTES

1. A typology of the most common flexible forms of employment applied in E.U. countries:

2. So, taking into consideration all the above information we can say that the relation between family and work covers a dimension which is deeply social, cultural, financial and political.

3. Gender inequality is considered to exercise direct discrimination in the participation of workers, in the fertility, the creation of a family and the quality of life. Issues such as working time, working conditions, lifelong learning, the benefits of the public sector – such as child care and the retirement system

Thoughts and Notes on the Issues of Reconciliation
of Work and Family Life in Europe.

49

– contribute to forming measures with the aim to better balance work and family life for all European citizens.

4. In general, all the European countries have stressed that the working hours of services (such as banks, shops, administrative authorities, the health system and schools) coincide with the working hours of the employees having as a result to make it more difficult to combine work and family life. Public services still operate with non-flexible working hours, while the working hours of shops have become more flexible under the pressure of consumers. In general, working hours are regulated by law, such as in Austria, Denmark, Spain, Greece and Italy, and this allowed their flexibility. In Austria all the more often once a week various services work more hours, as it happens, e.g. in the banking sector. Similarly, in Spain, some banks remain open in the evenings once a week. The same problem is also stressed in the case of the school hours. In Spain, as well as in Greece and Cyprus, a basic problem for parents is the fact that the school hours coincide with the working hours. As a result, in order to combine work and family life it is necessary not only to have certain statutory rules, but also to have the public care infrastructure that the State and the regions and local authorities ought to offer to the citizens in order to cover the care needs of the persons depending on them.

It is noted that at a community level there is a special legal text on child care, the Council Recommendation of the 31st of March 1992 *on child care*. As such, initiatives are undertaken with the aim to encourage the flexibility and diversity of child care services. Moreover, the possibility of access to child care services is encouraged, allowing to parents that work, to attend educational classes or vocational training classes in order to find a job or that are seeking a job, education or training with the aim to finding a job, to have access to local child care services. The services are offered at affordable prices for the parents, upon access to the services the needs of parents and children are being taken into consideration, there are available services at all areas and regions of the member states, in urban as well as in the rural areas, the services are accessible to children that have special needs. In Spain e.g. there is a big range of choices that in most case meet up to the special needs of the children and their parents. As such, flexibility and diversity are safeguarded, in which the *Recommendation on child care* explicitly refers to.

5. At the same time it is linked to the development of human resources, business profit, as well as the economic evolution, social cohesion and Democracy.

6. Several interesting proposals are submitted regarding the improvement of balancing family and professional life. Commissioner Amalia Sartori, for instance, in the Draft Report she submitted regarding the Roadmap for equality between men and women (2006-2010) in the frame of revision of policies of combining family and professional life proposes to the committee to "ensure that the cost of motherhood is borne not by business, but by society as a whole" (so as to eradicate discriminatory behaviour at work and help boost the birth rate), to "make care services and assistance to those who cannot look after themselves (children, people with disabilities, and the elderly) more accessible and flexible by laying down a minimum target for facilities remaining open at night so as to meet the needs arising from work and personal relationships" and "to lay down an initial form of compulsory paternity leave, amounting to 30 days". "The rapporteur suggests that each Member State appoint a national official to deal with equal opportunities issues, a *'Ms Lisbon'*, who, as the strategy is implemented and reviewed, should seek to bring about genuine gender mainstreaming in the implementing policies and keep political attention focused at all times on the matter of gender equality

7. But it is worth a remark: *Household Democracy* is not achieved through the one-sided female employment. Women need to be relieved from their multiple roles and share with their companions on a balanced basis the obligations and care duties within the family. This will allow them to utilize the skills, the talents and their experience and give a fresh impetus to the workplaces to the advantage of the society. At the same time men must deal more with their husband – parental role, actively participating in the democratic "administration" of their "family business". Husbands ought to become at last *"Equal Partners"*.

8. On this basis we distinguish four kinds of fatherhood: a) the biological fatherhood, which refers to a child's biological descent from a man, b) the legally recognised fatherhood, which defines fathers' rights and obligations based on the legislation and court decisions, c) the social fatherhood that recognises the role of the father to someone who shares their lives with a

Thoughts and Notes on the Issues of Reconciliation
of Work and Family Life in Europe.

51

child whether or not they are their biological fathers and d) the psychological fatherhood that refers to the close relationship a man develops with a child whether they live together or not.

9.The international bibliography points out the fact that both the concept of fatherhood and the ways that men behave as fathers has changed dramatically. The spearhead of these changes is what we traditionally refer to as "paternal responsibility". This responsibility now transcends the economic sphere, that is a man-father's obligation to satisfy the survival needs of the mother and children. In contemporary circumstances the role of the father becomes more "rounded", more "full", demanding the emotional support and coverage of the children and the mother apart from the economic responsibility

10. Especially in relation to the world of employers, it has already been made understood that work - life balance contributes to the decrease of differences that are connected to genders and to the improvement of quality in the working environment.

11. However the most important thing is that the policies of harmonizing family with career create win-win situations: a) the workers enjoy a better working environment and acquire greater satisfaction and self-esteem, b) the businesses benefit from the motivated and ambitious staff that is absent less and less from its work and that demonstrates higher productivity, c) harmonization helps in creating a flexible economy which uses constructively all its production staff.

12. As such, the harmonization measures of work / family life of the workers, that apply – or must be applied – in conjunction with other measures of social policy, must not simply constitute a solution for subsidy of businesses from the European Union in the framework of celebrating the "European Year of Equal Opportunities for All" (2007) , but to aim at developing the social awareness and the economy

PART II

≈

The Cypriot experience

CHAPTER 2.
THE PROBLEMATIC OF RECONCILIATION OF WORK AND FAMILY LIFE IN THE CYPRUS REPUBLIC

2.1. Generally

Cyprus is an independent state with more than 1.000.000 residents and it is the country with the higher female employment rate in the EU and with high educational level, at least in relation to women of the Greek-Cypriot group – they have important common points that are linked to their geography, the anthropogenic environment and their cultural background. And certainly, the field where this community expresses itself very intensely regards the social situation of women and in the relations amongst genders that continue to be determined by memories, behaviors and the value system of the powerful patriarchic past that historically flourished in the entire Mediterranean basin. Moreover, we must not ignore the close and complex relations of the area with the Muslim flows (but also the fact that Muslims constitute a part of their population even though they are absent from the Cypriot survey due to the "sensitive" intercommunal situation).

In Cyprus, despite the steps that have been made over the past years in the direction of increasing the number of women in political, social and financial decision-making centres, they are absent from the Council of Ministers, while the under-representation of women in respective bodies continues. In this country - an indicative reference is made - women (with exceptional presence in posts such as the Legislation Commissioner, the Ombudswoman, the Commissioner for the Protection of Personal Data and the Deputy Governor of the Central Bank of Cyprus etc) constitute 10.7% of the members of parliament, 3% of mayors, 17% of the members of municipal and community councils, 9.5% of teachers' trade union bodies etc. Recent studies have indicated that the Cypriot electorate does not trust women and strong traditional reflexes are found in the Cypriot society (obviously undermined in some cases, such as the impressive presence of women in the judicial body). They have also shown that both the educational system and the mass media, as well as the family, do not encourage the involvement of women in the political life and its processes. Consequently, Cyprus should intensify its efforts as a country, converging towards this direction with other EU countries, to encourage the participation of women in political, economic, social bodies and decision-making centers, and proceed to take measures to secure the preconditions that will allow involvement, in order to consider realistic and achieve the common aim of 30% of women's representation in the immediate future in all decision-making centers, thus winning significant points in altering the collective social conscience and changing the traditional/anachronistic stereotypes regarding the social roles of the genders.

It is well-known that the stereotypes are generalized models, with an intense evaluation nature, based on already formed judgments. They constitute preformed and simplified notions, socially accepted as correct or matter-of-fact. They are imposed through socialization and social control. The stereotypes linked to the social genders are a group of *"preformed and super-simplified social notions concerning the manner of behaviour, the skills, the roles, the professions etc of persons simply based on*

Thoughts and Notes on the Issues of Reconciliation
of Work and Family Life in Europe.

57

their gender." The social concepts-stereotypes regarding the genders are not restricted and do not only concern the personality traits, but also the roles that men and women take on and carry out within the family and extend to the workplace, the professions for which they are considered appropriate. An important part in reproducing and protracting these gender stereotypes is played by the mass media and the way they present women and especially female bodies. However, it is considered that the mass media, when encouraged - by following an ethics code regarding gender equality - can proceed with relative self-reforms and contribute to cultivating awareness, informing the public opinion and changing the anachronistic stereotypes. Already, since 2000, the EU is promoting the organization of information campaigns with the European mass media and events for the transnational exchange of information and determining and spreading good practices (such as an annual prize to companies and organizations that managed to promote equality between men and women) in order to strengthen the positive publicity of gender issues. Indeed, as proven by modern research, the area in which significant and broad changes could be made regarding gender stereotypes and the forming of a new type of social conscience, as already mentioned, is the area of education.

The above observations apply to Cyprus as well, where today a generalized effort is underway, led by the National Mechanism for Women's Rights, to inform and cultivate the awareness of the public opinion and social groups crucial for the promotion of equality, such as the workers and the owners of mass media, state officials, the Police, businesspeople etc, with a rich production of relative informative material. In this project, women's organizations, educational organizations, pioneering radio-television media etc can play an important role. It is obvious that in changing the patriarchal social models that have been in place for centuries, constitutes the total of aims and actions included in the current Plan. An even greater effort is needed in sectors that until now have not participated as dynamically as they should have in combating gender discrimination, such as parents and guardian organizations (since the family is a primary factor for the reproduction of traditional concepts linked to social genders) or self-administered organizations that express the local societies and their needs.

In Cyprus, for a great period of time there was a deficit of integrated policy in the sector of work - family life reconciliation. It is moreover worth noting that the lack of an integrated reconciliation policy was due to external factors, as to the absence until recently of a comprehensive, holistic – and not fragmentary – request for family-friendly policies during the procedure of collective bargaining, in conjunction with the obvious unwillingness and hesitation of the businesses to adopt family and women – friendly strategies. As there are no data arising from experience that interpret the phenomenon, we can hypothetically and only indicatively mention the following suspending factors that possibly applied in Cyprus:

(a) survival of the informal family support networks
(b) hesitation of the employers to offer their employees bigger flexibility regarding their working hours
(c) under-representation of women in collective bargaining
(d) particularly low percentage of women in the higher ranks of the trade union hierarchy
(e) lack of information regarding the applying family - friendly policies that apply in other European countries
(f) the fear of loss of income

Moreover, in relation to businesses, as relevant obstacles are considered:

- The high cost that these policies entail
- The prevailing culture and discourse uttered in its framework and as a result, the stance of the managers and executives
- The lack of staff containment policies
- The fact that the lifting of gender inequalities is not linked to economic growth and social cohesion.

Thoughts and Notes on the Issues of Reconciliation
of Work and Family Life in Europe.

59

We could talk about a kind of complacency that tends to be overcome, though, especially through the efforts of women themselves and their bodies (e.g. the National Mechanism for the Rights of Women, but also of other gender bodies) as well as the efforts undertaken by the EU and the Structural Funds with the indicative, under implementation, CI EQUAL. Moreover, today the respective awareness-raising is obvious and especially the trade unions that have included in their claims the issue of work family life reconciliation.

Over the past few years significant work has been done in Cyprus - mainly on an institutional level - regarding gender equality and lifting discriminations based on gender. An important push in this national, sociopolitical and economic aim was given by the country's accession to the European Union and the necessary harmonisation with the acquis communautaire, as well as the understanding of the fact that its successful economic grown, the high living standards of its inhabitants would not have been achieved without the active participation of half of its population, that is women.

The accumulated experience, especially in the field of legislation, the development of national mechanisms to promote the principles of gender equality, the active participation and contribution of women's organisations, the trade unions and other NGOs, formed the conditions for planning and implementing a "National Action Plan on the Equality of Men and Women", so that on the one hand Cyprus could participate in the generalised European effort to achieve gender equality, and on the other hand to promote the political, financial, social and cultural dimension of the effort and its direct link to the broader national efforts for growth and social cohesion. A precondition for the above was the approach of gender issues from the point of view of personal and social rights and the implementation of equality in all sectors of policy that had an impact on the daily life of women and men. The latter emerged from the fact that, despite the progress achieved on a legislation level, men and women continue to maintain asymmetric and prioritized relationships, both in the context of the family, as well as in the public sphere of life, that is in education/training, employment and entrepreneurship, representation in the social, political and financial decision-making centres etc. We should admit that in Cyprus as well the remnant position of women, both in the family and the society in general, is due to the unequal distribution of authority among the genders and the predetermination of gender social roles, which are the basis of discriminations.

What is the National Action Plan for Gender Equality.

It is a national plan which includes the framework strategy of the Republic of Cyprus for the incorporation of equality policies in all sectors, namely gender mainstreaming. Its main aim is *the modernization of the social model with an aim to utilize all human resources, irrespective of gender, and to eradicate all forms of discrimination against women.*

The expected results from its implementation focus on:

1. The evaluation of the response of implemented policies to the existing needs of women.
2. The increase of the percentage of women's employment.
3. The development of social infrastructure that will enhance the harmonization of professional and family responsibilities of men and women.
4. The change of attitude and stereotype notions regarding the social roles of the genders, through education, information/ awareness, changing the promotion of traditional models by the mass media, etc.
5. The improvement of sociopolitical conditions for the balanced participation of women in decision-making centers etc.

The Republic of Cyprus, adopting the principle of gender mainstreaming, is aiming through the current plan - through inter-complementary actions and positive actions - to promote gender equality in the economic, social and political life. So it is a horizontal nature

Thoughts and Notes on the Issues of Reconciliation
of Work and Family Life in Europe.

61

strategy, as the principle of mainstreaming demands. Main means of intervention are:

- The third and fourth Community Support Framework
- The community initiatives that have begun being implemented in Cyprus as well (Equal)
- The European experience (community framework strategies)
- The national acts

The current plan focuses on:

1. Promoting equality between men and women in the economic life and especially the labor market.
2. Promoting equality in education, training, science and research.
3. Promoting equal representation in the political, social and financial sector.
4. Combating all forms of direct or indirect violence against women and the gender-based trafficking of persons.
5. Promoting equal access to and equal implementation of social rights for men and women.
6. Changing the collective social conscience regarding stereotypes and prejudices lined to the social roles of the genders.

Regarding the Republic of Cyprus the increased number of women in the labour market in recent years constitutes an important development in the employment sector, since it resulted in raising their participation rates in the labour force at a local and European level. However, despite the progress that has been made, the labour market in Cyprus remains one of the harder fields of action for women, in comparison with men, as they are still burdened with the largest part of family responsibilities (e.g. children's upbringing and education, housework, care for any disabled family members or the elderly), whereas most businesses are still unwilling to consciously transcend the stereotypical conditions inside their environment – the so-called "sticky floor" or "glass ceiling" etc. (Dermanakis, 2004). However, in order to achieve the combination of family and professional life, but also economic growth and competitiveness, Cypriot businesses are invited to comply with the national and European policies of equality in employment – which in part aim, as mentioned before, at the combination of workers' family and professional life – to implement the relevant law provisions and to successfully deal with workers' demands in the frame of collective bargaining for the National General Collective agreement or the sectoral collective agreements.

2.2. *A good practice in Cyprus: Project "Open Doors"*

In Cyprus over the past few years a broad debate is being held regarding corporate social responsibility at the initiative of the Employers' and Industrialists' Federation of Cyprus (OEB), which has caused great interest. However, the gender dimension in this context remains very weak. Cypriot businesspeople to one degree or the other still do not fully understand the importance of equality strategies and are not yet willing to link them to their social responsibility or their business profit. This was one of the main causes for the planning and implementation of the actions of project "Open Doors" of Development Partnership ELANI for the reconciliation of the professional and family life of the workers and above all the women. One of the main actions was the forming of a new professional profile, that of the Equality Adviser, in the Cypriot labor market, with the relevant training and awareness of 25 officers of the public sector mainly and of businesses, trade unions and educational organizations etc. After their long training - which made them able to plan inter-business equality strategies with emphasis on those for reconciliation - the trainees proceeded to plan and implement Reconciliation Plans in businesses that accepted to cooperate with Development Collaboration ELANI. Based on the taught methodology that allowed:

- Defining the profile of the business

Thoughts and Notes on the Issues of Reconciliation
of Work and Family Life in Europe.

63

- Recording the status of working women and the problems they are facing regarding their family obligations
- Recording the views of the workers regarding their needs and the potential of the business to contribute towards covering them
- Processing the results that will emerge from the respective surveys in order to form a complete picture of the measures that a business should take in order to better promote the Reconciliation of Professional and Family Life
- Identifying the action spans and the planning and prioritization of actions
- Creating a data base or a documentation centre for monitoring and evaluating the implemented measures and policies
- Forming proposals for the implementation of specific interventions and the implementation of measures to promote reconciliation, monitoring and evaluation of the interventions, in order to support the forming of future actions.

A series of innovative activities was implemented aiming during the first stage at cultivating the awareness of the employers and the employees by bringing the issue of reconciliation to the centre of inter-business discussions, linking it with the corporate social responsibility and the business profit, and in several cases leading to specific proposals, as well as promoting relative good practices. Participating in the action were organisations of the public sector (e.g. Ayios Athanasios Municipality of Limassol and the Cyprus Police Academy) and businesses (hotel, private education organization, retail shop etc). In all the organization a small survey was held to determine the stance and the mood, and a short seminar was held to cultivate the awareness of the male staff - irrespective of professional status and capacity - titled *"modern necessity to redistribute the social roles within the family as a main precondition for achieving reconciliation."*

The surveys of mood and stance gave interesting data for the mediation of gender in labor procedures and the way men and women experience the workplace, the work time and the working conditions, as well as the crucial relationship between family and professional life. An indicative example is the results of the survey carried out among workers at a local administration organization (the sample comprised 35% men and 65% women):

- There is still to a great extent a deficit in the distribution of roles in the life of the couple.
- A serious factor of the deficit in reconciling the family and professional life is the lack of social welfare structures.
- There is still to quite a great extent a dependence of the reproduction family on the orientation family.
- Women especially would be satisfied with flexible forms of employment.

While on the contrary on a business level, where the sample comprised women only, it appeared that the working women with the responsibility of dependant persons in conditions of full employment refused part-time employment and none of them wanted to work less hours. At the same time they do not consider that they are facing any great problem of contributing to the care of dependant members by their husbands/partners, since 83% contribute practically and 75% contribute financially too. And the specific women said that their most serious problem was the lack of relevant structures and the cost of the existing ones.

However, from the survey that took place in the research department of a large educational organization of tertiary private education, which examined the views of women researchers, that is persons with high scientific qualifications, it emerged that in infant care, child care after school, care for the elderly, transportation of children to school, transportation of children to private lessons, homework, children's medical care, elderly parents' medical care, communication with teachers, child care during school holidays, shopping for children's needs, movement/entertainment of elderly parents, entertainment of

Thoughts and Notes on the Issues of Reconciliation
of Work and Family Life in Europe.

65

children, a percentage of 30% to 50% in all cases said it is undertaken by the mother and 8% to 16% by the mother and father. The average that stated this is undertaken by the father is about 9%.

During the seminars to cultivate the awareness of male workers - which one should note was the first to be carried out in Cyprus and indeed simultaneously in over ten organizations in various areas - in which about 200 people participated, there were restrained reactions to the dominant argumentation of the *"natural destiny of the genders"*. The most interesting was that the most intense reactions were among young people of a high educational level studying in the Police Academy.

The specific activity was concluded by submitting certain small but significant proposals by the new Equality Advisers both to the organizations and D.C. ELANI, which include pancyprian research and the notification of their results to the state, the employer/trade union organizations, equality organizations etc, actions of broad publicity and social awareness, with emphasis on the employers, studies to create childcare structures within the organizations etc. Especially noted is the complete survey to create a Centre for the Creative Occupation of Children implemented by the Ayios Athanasios Municipality advisers with the contribution of the scientific head of project Open Doors, which was accepted by the Mayor and will soon operate at the under construction multipurpose centre of the municipality. It will not only address the staff but also the inhabitants. Also noted is the production of an exceptional DVD with the good practices regarding gender equality and equal opportunities emerging from the implementation of an open doors system with the very obvious gender dimension exercised at one of the biggest and oldest hotels of Limassol, Holiday Inn. It is not by chance, of course, that its owner is a member of Cyprus' women's movement and is active in the Mechanism for Women's Rights and that the personnel manager was trained as an equality adviser. The DVD, sponsored by the National Administrative Authority of C.P. EQUAL, will be distributed to all Cypriot businesses. Some of the actions of project "Open Doors" of Development Partnership ELANI for the reconciliation of the professional and family life of the workers and above all the women are:

2.3. *Planning inter-business equality strategies with emphasis on the reconciliation/harmonization of the family and professional life*

In planning and implementing reconciliation policies, experience from the implementation of equality policies could prove to be very useful. Equality schemes have already been implemented and evaluated in Greece with the contribution of Equal programmes, such as "Andromeda" programme. In the Manual for the Implementation of Equality Plans,(Liapi and Tzavara, 2005) utilize some already existing surveys to present a typological form of equality actions. These actions are categorized in the first unit with the criterion being their content, and in the second unit with the criterion being the procedures and the manner of implementation followed. In brief, we mention that, according to their content the equality actions could be:

1. Focused on and addressing only one group of the population.
2. Sporadic or scattered and implemented in different issues and different sectors of the population. These actions, if there is a comprehensive equality strategy, can act as a means for spreading the experience. On the other hand, there is the danger of the actions canceling one another.
3. Multilevel or crosswise actions. They can be implemented by organizations already orientated towards equality and which have adopted a holistic approach in this direction.

At the same time, if we categorize the equality actions according to the procedures and manner of implementation, we can speak about:

1. The focused or "one off" approach, that is the methodical and detailed approach implemented in one action only.

Thoughts and Notes on the Issues of Reconciliation
of Work and Family Life in Europe.

67

2. The structural approach, which is characterized by medium-term planning and aims at more permanent result. This approach is implemented when the results of the actions are monitored, when the actions are coherent and complete, and a multiplying/increasing result is guaranteed.

3. The continuous approach, which is characterized by long-term aims and prospects and has to do with the cases of organizations that have incorporated equality in their policies, procedures, practices and culture.

Respectively, the expected results of these actions are categorized. The focused actions are expected to have restricted results and constitute an initial level regarding equality policies. The scattered actions, which are based on the structured approach, are expected to have sporadic results and involve an interim stage, while the multilevel actions and continuous methodology lead to comprehensive and diffused results that describe an advanced logic of implementing equality policies and adapting the functioning of organizations to its principles.

In Greece and Cyprus, the integration of equality policies and specifically policies for the reconciliation of professional and family life are at a primary stage. It is understandable that the first actions proposed are focused on specific measures and social structures (for example the implementation of a social timetable in social child care and care for the elderly structures, through a focused methodology that studies the parametres of the specific or other focused actions in depth, as it emerges from the Cypriot experience of pilot implementations in businesses and organisations, and even in the local administration). However, it is important when planning reconciliation policies to aim at an advanced state, where in the end its reason and necessity will be clear and will hold a leading role in political decisions, the ways social structures function and the attitude of the citizens. Something like this could be achieved with the systematic evaluation of our interventions with these criteria and their improvement in this direction.

Irrespective of their composition and the focus of their actions, both the Greek D.P. INTERVENTION and the Cypriot D.P. ELANI that participate in Transnational Collaboration SEMELI believe that the redistribution of social roles in the family and the reconciliation of family and professional life are fundamental factors for achieving gender equality and equal opportunities, and that the participation of businesses in the whole project is a turning point. So, wanting to promote the significance of the participation of businesses in balancing the professional life of women, mainly, and men, we will try to present here an action plan, utilizing the pilot implementation of Equality Plans in the context of *"Equal - Andromeda"*, as it is codified in the "Manual for the implementation of Equality Plans" by Maria Liapi and Maria Tzavara, as well as the previously mentioned Cypriot experience and the educational material and tools produced in its context.

In general, the contribution of businesses to reconciliation can be implemented through:

- Extending parental leave
- The right to paternal leave being equal to maternity leave.
- Sponsoring a child station
- Respect of the timetable of workers
- Disconnecting professional advancement from family obligations
- In general the implementation of gender mainstreaming in the operation of the business.

The aim is to adopt a specific methodology that will allow:

- Defining the business profile. Recording the status of the women workers and the problems they are facing regarding their family obligations.
- Recording the views of the workers regarding their needs and the possibility of the contribution of the business to cover them.
- Processing the results that will emerge from the respective surveys in order to form a complete picture of the measures

Thoughts and Notes on the Issues of Reconciliation
of Work and Family Life in Europe.

69

that a business should take for the best possible promotion of the Work-Family Life Balance.

- Identifying the action fronts and the planning and prioritization of specific actions.
- Creating a database or a documentation unit to monitor and evaluate the implemented measures and policies.
- Drafting proposals for the implementation of specific interventions and the implementation of measures to promote reconciliation monitor and evaluate interventions, so that the forming of future actions can be supported.

In other words it is a process respective to that which is proposed to be followed by the local administrations and the public benefit businesses, on the side of the companies planning the support of their workers.

The factors of traits of the businesses changing the attraction strategies and the form of interventions to follow could be the size and number of employees, the sector of the business, its legal form (public/private), the degree of development potential of the sector or the business, the degree of awareness regarding corporate social responsibility issues etc. The intervention fronts regarding the reconciliation of professional and family life mainly concern leave, the provision of services and allowances. Specifically (Liapi,&. Tzavara, 2005):

- Leave more favorable than that provided for by the law, such as extending the legal duration of maternity leave, establishing the right for accumulated parental leave (9 months), flexible leave, reduced working hours for pregnant women and/or facilities for more flexible ways to regulate their working time, arrangement of the working time for mothers.
- Establishment of special paid leave, such as leave in case of illness of dependant members, extra paid leave to monitor the school performance of children for men and women.

- Provision of family support services, vocational orientation, financial support, consultative services etc. Specifically, allowances for childcare services, such as allowance for single mothers, financial support of childcare expenses, reduction of the working hours by two hours and/or the sponsoring of parents of children with special needs, free transportation on public transport etc. Furthermore, the creation and operation of infant and child stations either within the business premises or in cooperation with public/private/municipal services, joining the programme "Help at Home" etc.

- Actions to cultivate awareness and provide information within and outside the environment of the business. It is expected that there will be an information deficit regarding equality issues in general and the pilot reconciliation programme specifically. Also, it is often observed that within businesses there is reduced internal communication among the various hierarchical levels. In this context, a series of measures and actions is proposed for information and awareness, addressed to all workers, candidates for employment and officers of all degrees, trade union organizations, the workers' representatives etc.

The methodology of planning, monitoring and evaluating reconciliation plans

As already mentioned in relation to the local administrations, a precondition to implement a comprehensive policy on reconciliation is primarily to investigate the needs of the workers in every business. Also needed is the commitment of the business on a high administrative level, so that the specific proposals to be made do not sink. It is also necessary to appoint a specially trained person, aware of gender equality and equal opportunities issues, to be in charge of implementing the actions (the equality officer and/or the equality adviser). In this way, the businesses welcome and incorporate in their workforce a new professional capacity,

Thoughts and Notes on the Issues of Reconciliation
of Work and Family Life in Europe.

71

that of the equality adviser, which already in Greece is offered as a post-graduate by the Aegean University. Finally, it is necessary to obtain the active commitment of all involved parties, workers' representatives, men and women, management etc. The inflow of know-how is necessary for the planning and implementation of interventions through their cooperation with specialized equality organizations and experts. It is also necessary to develop a system to monitor and evaluate the results of the actions by establishing criteria that seriously take into consideration the gender dimension.

Steps towards taking measures with an aim to promote reconciliation

1. Preparation of the business profile (number of male and female employees, needs, jobs, timetables, contracts etc)
2. Investigation of the special needs in relation to family life through interviews and questionnaires (see ANNEX 1). At the end of this phase it must be made known which issues concerning the balancing of the family and professional life concern the workers and possibly restrict the possibilities of women to participate on an equal basis.
3. Forming specific proposals that will gradually improve the conditions and will form a family-friendly working environment. These proposals must be made in agreement with managerial officers and be accepted on a high level, in order to prevent any obstacles in their foreseen implementation.
4. At every stage of planning and implementation, detailed reports are necessary to describe in detail the criteria, the steps and the positive results of the action, as well as possible difficulties that may have arisen.
5. Every successful intervention must be publicized so that the intervention is made known, so that it acts in a multiplying

way in the business sector and helps change the attitude, the workers, the business world and the society in general.

6. Based on the existing experience, at the end of each programming period the results are evaluated and new aims are set, so that the business can reach a very high level in the sector of equality, its vehicle being the policies for the reconciliation of professional and family life.

Through the evidence mentioned and also the utilization of the huge wealth of good practices from the European experience on a corporate level, it is possible for the Greek businesses, public and private, to play a leading role in the progress of the society, the improvement of the quality of life of the citizens, and at the same time enhancing the productivity and quality of their work.

2.4. *Charting of gender social map of the Cyprus Republic*

Scientific Head of Project: Maria Gasouka
Head of Research: Chrystalla A. Ellinas

In a recent resolution, the EU Council and the European ministers of labor and social policy (Official Journal of the European Communities 2000/C218/02) call on the member states to form a group of proposals for measures to achieve the balanced undertaking of family responsibilities concerning dependant persons by working men and women. Spot-on, the resolution points out the network of anachronistic concepts and stereotypes that urge men in many even European societies to consciously or unconsciously avoid taking paternal leave and in this way stay away from their children and families (K.E.Θ.I. 2007) and determines as especially important two spheres of social policy and interventions: a) the further strengthening of child and elderly care networks, and b) the promotion on behalf of the businesses of family-friendly policies. Both the redistribution of social roles of the genders and the reconciliation strategies that should be

Thoughts and Notes on the Issues of Reconciliation
of Work and Family Life in Europe.

73

planned and implemented by the state and the businesses are at the centre of attention of the project Open Doors, and the philosophy that supports the forming of the "Gender Charter of the Republic of Cyprus".

The specific study is a significant action of the project "Open Doors", which was designed and implemented by Development Collaboration ELANI, co-funded by the Republic of Cyprus (50%) and the European Social Fund (50%) in the framework of Community Initiative EQUAL. It reflects and expresses the feminist ideology of the project and its conclusions fully justified the choice of aims and pursuits, as well as the necessity for the actions (sub-projects) chosen to be relevantly developed. It also constitutes an important tool of knowledge and understanding of the modern Cypriot society and from this point of view will be very useful in the future for anyone who wishes to utilize it in studies, and thus contribute to the viability of the project.

One of the aims of Barcelona (2002) and the European Employment Strategy is to achieve a better combination of professional and private life through the increase of child care services by 2010. The specific aims set out the coverage of at least 90% of children aged three till the beginning of schooling, and at least 33% of the children under three years of age. In Cyprus, even though the National Action Plan for Employment (NAPE) 2004-2006 refers to these European aims, it only adopted the first of these as a national aim for children aged three till the beginning of schooling. It did not set an aim regarding children under the age of three, alleging a lack of data "for the needs of families with children of this age" (National Action Plan for Employment 2004-2006). However, it waited for a pan cyprian study to be carried out to determine the social needs and "future setting of aims in the specific sector of children" (National Action Plan for Employment 2004-2006). NAPE refers to figures provided by the Statistical Service (2002/2003) which during the time the Plan was being drafted showed an 82% coverage in Cyprus for children aged three till obligatory schooling. For children under three years of age, the coverage was 12%.

The very low aim for children under three years of age, both on a national and European level, indicates the existence of other informal care forms at home, such as care by grandparents, house maid, or outside the house such as paid care by women at their own home. Also, it indicates the stance of various cultural groups regarding their preferred type of care for small children and the varying forms and duration of mother, father and parental leave existing in the member states. Only five member states have managed to meet the Barcelona aim with 33% of coverage for children less than three years of age (Belgium, Denmark, France, Sweden and The Netherlands). In many countries, the percentage of coverage is under 10%, such as Spain, Austria, the Czech Republic, Germany, Greece, Lithuania, Italy, Hungary and Poland (European Commission, 2005)[1]. The percentage in Cyprus for covering children less than three years of age is around the same low levels (12%) with the percentages of the aforementioned group of states (Statistical Service 2002/03). However, the differences are tremendous compared to the Scandinavian countries, where childcare is considered to be a social right (Denmark, Finland, Sweden). Specifically, in Sweden the child care services cover 45% of children aged one and 86% of children aged two to five. For every child aged four, free pre-school education is provided. The recent determination of the highest level for the cost of childcare had direct results in increasing the already high percentage of women's employment (European Commission, 2005 αλλά και Fagan and Hebson, 2004). Although the Scandinavian countries offer a different picture, especially compared to the Mediterranean countries, we notice a convergence in the EU regarding some statistical data (Fagan and Hebson 2004):

- The percentage of employment for women with young children is 13.6% lower compared to the percentage of women without children
- The percentage of men with young children is 10% higher in relation to that of men without children

Thoughts and Notes on the Issues of Reconciliation
of Work and Family Life in Europe.

75

In Cyprus, the *National Action Plan on Equality* (2006) incorporates the Barcelona aims (2002) for the percentages of child care services in the context of the first aim, which is "the promotion of equality between men and women in the economic life and especially in the labour market area". The Plan proposes specific actions for its implementation:

- "Recording and upgrading the existing structures for child care and care for the elderly. Creation of new ones in the centre and regions. Adaptation of the operation terms and provision of services to the needs of the workers, according to the pursuits of the National Action Plan for Employment.

- Establishment of motives so that the businesses proceed with actions to create a business environment that will be women-friendly - Establishment of an annual relevant award" (National Action Plan for Equality, 2006).

Apart from the incorporation of the Barcelona aims (2002), both the National Action Plan for Equality and the National Action Plan for Employment respond to the specific gender gap of employment in the EU and Cyprus. If the percentage of women's employment is considered to be high because it almost reaches the Lisbon aims (60%), it is far from the employment percentage of men (80%). According to the latest EUROSTAT figures, Cyprus presents the largest gap in pay between men and women (25%), while the average in the EU25 is 15%. Even though the gap remains wide, there appears to be a reduction. The difference was 33% ten years ago, in 1999 it dropped to 27% and in 2004 to 25%. Only 13.6% of Cypriot women is represented in administrative positions, with the lowest percentage in the EU25, which is under half of the average in the EU, which is 32.1%/ Apart from Malta (15%), which is on a similar level with Cyprus, the next country with the lowest percentage is Denmark with 23%. Regarding the remaining statistics, which draw the profile of women's employment, Cyprus shows a higher percentage of unemployment among women (6.4%) in relation to men (4.5%), and a professional differentiation in employment. These differences appear in almost all the other countries of the EU. However, the statistics that show Cyprus as a leader of the rear-guard in Europe were broadly publicized by the media after the EUROSTAT figures and the Commission's annual report on the labor market were released in the context of implementing the Lisbon aims. The publication in the press happened just before the World Women's Day with titles such as "Cypriot women, the most hard done by in the EU".

The European Directives relating to the issue of reconciliation of professional-personal life, such as parental leave, part-time employment, maternity and work time organization, have been incorporated in the national policy during the country's harmonization with the acquis communautaire. The harmonization introduced many new norms (parental leave) and in other cases amended existing legislation (maternity). The proposal to amend the Directive on Working Time could bring about important changes, because it proposes the worker's right to adjust their working hours to better combine their professional and private life.

With Cyprus' accession to the EU, mobility is apparent regarding equality issues between men and women. This mobility emerges from the necessary implementation of directives and Community processes, such as the European Strategy on Employment, the drawing of funds from the Structural Funds and generally from all the obligations of an EU member state. The National Action Plans 2004-06 for Employment, Social Integration and Gender Equality introduce policies, aims, actions and ideas that in many cases are pioneering for the Cypriot social policy. The European Commission takes into consideration the evaluations of the National Plans by independent experts, with the setting up of teams of experts. Regarding Cyprus, the first National Action Plans 2004-06 for Employment and Social Integration received broad and important reviews concerning gender prospects (Panayiotou 2004a, 2004b, 2004c).

Thoughts and Notes on the Issues of Reconciliation
of Work and Family Life in Europe.

77

The post-accession mobility is also apparent in the research activity in Cyprus and the participation of many institutions in various programmes co-funded by the EU:

- Programmes of Aim 3 European Social Fund (ESF)[2]
- Community Initiatives *EQUAL* [3]
- Fifth and Sixth Framework Programme of the European Union[4]

Very important studies have been completed by trade unions and employer's organizations. The Employers and Industrialists Federation (OEB), apart from its multiple participation in the Community Initiatives *EQUAL,* has concluded two very important gallops. The first pan cyprian study regarding "The position of women in the modern Cypriot business" (2004) aimed at pin-pointing the percentage of participation in various sectors and the reasons for low participation. One of the conclusions of the study was the very low percentage of women's participation in managerial positions. This specific result and its concerns regarding the issue was the reason for conducting a second study to better focus on the reasons of women's absence from managerial positions in two sectors of the economy (OEB 2005).[5] One of the results announced is that: "The main reason that restricts women's participation in higher management positions is family obligations and stereotypes" (OEB 2005). Other recent gallops in Cyprus were conducted by the Department of Women workers of PEO trade union (2004) titled *"Provision of facilities to working parents: The role of the state and the local administration".* The study was pan cyprian and covered households with mothers up to 55 years of age with children aged 4 months to 16 years. Finally, the women's organization of the Democratic Party (GODIK) conducted a study on the reconciliation of family-professional life and its results were presented in March 2006.

Through the aforementioned studies, the inequality of men and women in businesses, public organizations and within the family in Cyprus has begun being recorded. So far we did not have any information regarding the implementation of special measures on the reconciliation of family-professional life and the child care services on the employers' level. Reports to the Commission refer to the absence of measures on the level of organizations and businesses (Panayiotou 2004c). However, a pioneering measure, unique for Cypriot standards, was implemented with great success and no advertising whatsoever by maritime company Interorient Navigation Co. Ltd. (INC), in Limassol. Two-and-a-half years ago, Interorient established an all-day free-of-charge nursery station for employees' children. Further down we will refer in detail to the content of the interview I had with Mrs. Alexia Papadopoulou, Legal Advisor of INC Company.[6] The case of Interorient provides multiple lessons for researchers, employers and state authorities alike. This case could be used as an example of a measure and a model for the reconciliation of family-professional life in Cyprus.

CASE STUDY: INTERORIENT

Mrs. Papadopoulou, the only woman on the Board of Directors of Interorient, undertook to materialize the idea of the Chairman of the Board, Mr. Adonis Papadopoulos, for the establishment of a nursery station for the children of the company's employees. Mr. A. Papadopoulos knew that such measures had been implemented in companies abroad and that the issue of caring for pre-school age children caused problems to his employees. The problem was especially apparent for the women workers regarding the specific timetable of the company (9am - 6pm with a one-hour break at noon) and the public or private nursery schools.7 He was "a strong supporter of the idea" and positively influenced the other members of the Board with his enthusiasm. Mrs. Alexia Papadopoulou admitted she was the only one who had some reservations, not about the idea itself, but regarding the huge responsibility for the safety and education of the children that the company would bear. She herself, through personal experience in taking care of her own children knew the difficulties of combining a

Thoughts and Notes on the Issues of Reconciliation
of Work and Family Life in Europe.

79

professional life with child care very well. The idea was not discussed with the staff at all, which never made a demand to the management to discuss the issue.

After a Board decision, Mrs. Alexia Papadopoulou undertook the relevant research to implement the decision, which concerned specialised issues of setting up a nursery station, finding staff and a place. Mrs. Papadopoulou claimed that the financial cost was not a negative factor for implementation, since the decision of the Board was based on and in accordance with the general philosophy of the company, which sees the staff not only as dynamic and productive, but also as a receiver of services from the company. Apart from the nursery station, the company offers a daily free meal to its staff in the building's canteen during the one-hour lunch break.

After many preparations, the hiring of staff, approvals by state services of the Ministry of Education, the Welfare Office, the Fire Department etc, the station, called *"The Little Magic Boat"*, operated in 2004 exclusively for the children of the company's employees. Attendance was free for children aged three months to five years that is from the time maternity leave ends up to the obligatory pre-school education. Due to specifications of the Ministry of Education, the station cannot include pre-school education for children aged five to six yet. However, there are future plans for the station to offer pre-school education. Free attendance is offered to all the children of the specified ages and covers lunch and other extra activities, such as outings, shows etc. Usually the cost for such activities is not covered even in public or community nursery schools. In many cases, up to two children of a worker attend the station at the same time. The station has a total of six employees for 35 children, of which four are qualified nursery school teachers, one caretaker, and one administrative officer. Since the station opened, the number of children is around the same level, with infants taking the place of children who leave for pre-school education. The timetable of the station reflects the timetable of the company (9am -

6pm) with half an hour extra before work starts and half an hour after the working day is over, that is 8.30am - 6.30pm.

For the time being, the station is not within the premises of the building due to lack of space. Mrs. Papadopoulou showed me the blueprints of the new building, which will host the company and includes a huge area for a nursery school of very high specifications. This practical planning proves not only the long-term commitment of the company to this institution, but also its dedication to continue offering high quality care. The quality of the service provided is also proven by the fact that parents who are not working for Inteorient have asked to be allowed to bring their children to the station due to the fame it has acquired in the short time it has been operating. However, the regulations of the station forbid the attendance of other children, apart from those whose parents work for the company or the station. The quality of care provided by the station is verified by two other workers, with whom I have talked. They have also stressed the huge financial benefit for a family with two children from the operation of the station, which could reach 50% or more of the salary of a low income worker.

This pioneering measure is unique for Cypriot standards, not only in the private sector, but also in the public sector. Higher public and private educational institutions offering nursery schooling could organise nursery schools much easier to cover the needs of workers. These institutions have the teaching staff and with the obligatory practical work of students could offer high quality care at a low cost. The provision of this care by Inteorient is not only pioneering for Cyprus, but also for Europe due to the fact that it is totally free and fully covers all the children from infancy. Many European public and private organisations, offering such services to their workers, are based on fees which may be funded to some extent and restrict the total number of children, as well as the age of attendance. For example, a large organisation of the European Union, such as the European Development Bank, offers care for children of a pre-school age with fees reaching 10% of the monthly

Thoughts and Notes on the Issues of Reconciliation
of Work and Family Life in Europe.

81

salary of the worker and a maximum of 700-800 euros per month for all-day schooling. Furthermore, there is a restriction on the number of children and the age of attendance.

Many private organisations in the EU have implemented policies for equal opportunities, reconciliation of professional-family life and integration of social groups which are excluded from the labour market. Apart from the moral and legal reasons, these organisations have used these policies to advertise the company, promoting specific business aims, and have evaluated these actions based on the economic benefit they will bring about (European Commission. 2005c). A study in the framework of the European Action Plan on Eliminating Discrimination 2001-2006, which covered the 25 member states, focused on the evaluation of benefits to be brought about by the integration of equality strategies in businesses, and presents many examples of "Good Practices" in many large organizations, such as Ford, Deutche Telekom, Deutche Bank, Tesco, Shell and IBM in the United Kingdom and Germany (European Commission. 2005c). Interorient, although the only case we find in Cyprus, did not use some form of promoting the company's image. The free nursery school is not listed in the company's brochures or its website, but is merely mentioned to the candidates for new jobs. In her interview, Mrs. Papadopoulou expressed her personal view that any benefits could not cover the huge cost of the nursery school. Irrespective of the results, the company will continue this institution. In any case, there are no plans for the evaluation of benefits.

CHAPTER 3.
THE RESEARCH

⁓

3.1. *The identity of the research*

population:

Workers, men and women, with dependant persons in the three largest urban centers (Nicosia, Limassol, Larnaca) in economic activities in which both genders are represented.8

methodology:

Random layered sampling. The sample is relative to the workers in each area and in each economic activity, according to the figures of the Workforce Study.

method of sampling:

Self-completed written questionnaires without supervision and the presence of an interviewer, which were distributed at workplaces by the members of the three organisations of the sub-project group: Union of Bank Employees of Cyprus (ETYK), Employers and Industrialists Federation (OEB) and Cyprus Gender Equality Observatory (PIK).

size of sample:

300 persons

Thoughts and Notes on the Issues of Reconciliation
of Work and Family Life in Europe.

83

period of research:
10/4/2006-28/4/2006

scientific head of project:
Maria Gasouka
head of research:
Chrystalla A. Ellinas

sub-project team:
Joseph Anastasiou (PIK), Christina Vassila (OEB) and Mimis Theodotou
(ETYK) in cooperation and communication with scientific head of
Research Dr. Maria Gasouka.

The aims of the research are to determine:

1. "the social situation of Cypriot women in the labor market",
2. "the relationship of this situation with the distribution of inter-
   family duties and obligations, among the two genders", and
3. "its consequences on professional expectations and taking of
   relevant decisions by women (workers, unemployed, those
   who never worked with relation to dependant work or self-
   employment in the public sphere of life)"

Specifically, with the quantitative research the following was
charted:

- discrimination and inequality of working time and care of men
  and women within the family
- perceptions, notions, image of self etc of workers - unemployed
  - "traditionally" unemployed women, in relation to the dilemma
  family-professional obligations, especially in areas such as self-
  guilt, resignation, stress etc.
- Perceptions, notions, "image of self" etc of men working in
  businesses regarding the integration of Equality Strategies in their
  operation and the possibility of implementing "Reconciliation
  Frameworks" of family-professional life and workers".

The questionnaire was drafted based on the aims set out in the Technical Bulletin of the Sub-project. The head of research submitted a preliminary questionnaire to the team as a basis for discussion. For comparative purposes and in order to examine tools already used, we contacted the head of the European Social Survey to use questions from the alternating unit (G1 - G124), *Family, work and prosperity, Work-life equilibrium*, European Social Survey 2004/05). This pan-European survey is carried out every two years and covers 20 countries. The first round was carried out in 2002/2003 and the second in 2004/2005. The programme is funded by the European Commission, the European Science Foundation and academic national organizations in every participating country. The national research organization in charge in Greece is the National Centre for Social Surveys, which uses the common questionnaire, translated into Greek. A European Social Survey researcher at the City University told us that, even though there was interest by people in Cyprus, they could not find the necessary national organizations to co-fund the project. The absence of Cyprus from this pan-European project leaves a huge gap in collecting data in the field of comparative politics and sociology. Some of the questions of the unit *Work-life equilibrium* were partially adopted and implemented for the needs of our questionnaire (See questionnaire ELANI, questions 11, 13, 14, 15, 21, 24, 25, 26, 27). This research was conducted between 10-28 April, among men and women workers with dependant persons in the three largest urban centres (Nicosia, Limassol, Larnaca) in the economic activities in which both genders are represented. The economic activities not included due to unsatisfactory representation of both genders are: agriculture, fishing, mining and construction. Furthermore, the categories "other services", private households and exterritorial organizations were excluded (Workforce Survey, 2004).

The methodology implemented is random layered sampling. The sample is relative to the workers in each district and in each economic activity, according to figures of the Workforce Survey. Self-completed written questionnaires without supervision and the presence of an

Thoughts and Notes on the Issues of Reconciliation
of Work and Family Life in Europe.

85

interviewer were distributed in the workplaces by the members of the three organizations of the sub-project team: ETYK, OEV and PIK. The size of the sample was 300 persons, out of which 272 returned completed questionnaires (91%). Of these, 54% where from the Nicosia district, 31% from Limassol and (N=269) from Larnaca.

3.2. Demographic characteristics of sample

Gender, age and marital status

Men represent 36% of the sample and women 63% (N=253). The reason for the high representation of women compared to the employment percentage of the population is the disproportional representation of the professional category "Secretary/Cashier" with 24.7% of the sample. In this category, there is an obvious gender separation, where 93.8% of those asked are women and only 6.3% are men.

The average age of those asked is 38, the lowest being 20 years and the highest 59 years (N= 261). The highest percentage is found in the category of 31-40 years of age (44%), followed by the category of 41-59 years of age (35%) and the lowest percentage in the ages 20-30 (21%).

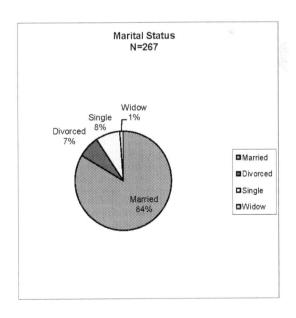

Marital Status
N=267

Widow
1%
Single
8%
Divorced
7%
Married
84%

Married
Divorced
Single
Widow

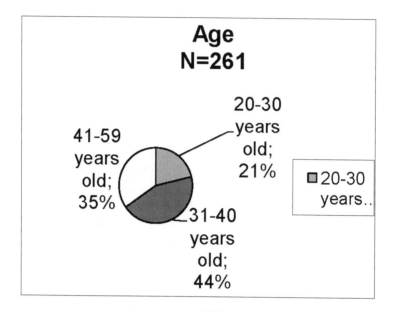

Regarding the marital status, the majority of workers with dependants (82%). The divorced are 7%, single 8%, and widows/widowers 1% (N=267).

The majority of those asked belong to households where both spouses work (85%, N=240).

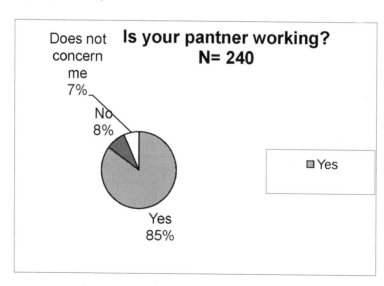

Thoughts and Notes on the Issues of Reconciliation
of Work and Family Life in Europe.

87

Sector of work, profession and education

In the public and semi-governmental sector and in local administration, we find 26% of the sample, while 71% is in the private sector.

Work sector		N	%	Valid %
Valid	Public, semi-governmental, local administration	71	26.1	26.3
	Private	191	70.2	70.7
	Other	8	2.9	3.0
	Total	270	99.3	100.0
Void	.	2	0.7	
Total		272	100.0	

The horizontal and vertical separation into professional categories reveals the gender form of employment. The horizontal division is obvious with the gathering of women in the profession "Secretary/Cashier". Among women, 37.5% say they belong to this professional category, while only 4.4% of men said the same. Among men, the technical staff, workers and drivers make up 22% compared to only 5.6% among women. The vertical gender separation becomes apparent through the comparison of two professional categories which are at the same time in opposite hierarchical grades. While 27.5% among men said they hold managerial positions, only 8.8% of women are on the same level. The situation is reversed in the lower hierarchical grade of secretaries and cashiers with 37.5% of women compared to only 4.4% of men.

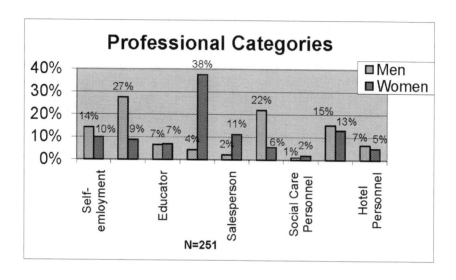

Education

The level of education for more than half of the women of the sample is high school (57.6%), followed by the university level as the second highest percentage (29.1%). For men, the percentage in secondary and higher education is almost equal, with 43% having finished high school and 42% university.

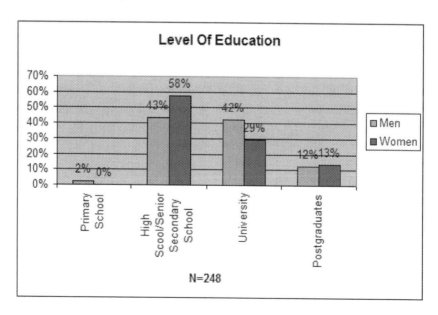

Thoughts and Notes on the Issues of Reconciliation
of Work and Family Life in Europe.

89

Number of children

Half of those asked (50.6%) have two children, 26% have only one child and 13% three children.

Number of children		N	%	Valid %
Valid	Without children	16	5.9	6.2
	1 child	67	24.6	26.1
	2 children	130	47.8	50.6
	3 children	35	12.9	13.6
	More than 3 children	9	3.3	3.5
	Total	257	94.5	100.0
Void	.	15	5.5	
Total		272	100.0	

Regarding the ages of the children, most of those asked have children in primary school (45%). The next categories are shared equally between children of pre-school age (34%), high school (32%) and higher education (36%).

Children/Dependants	Percentage %
Pre-school age	34
Primary school	45
High school	32
Higher education	36
Army	4
Adults	10

3.3. Distribution of inter-family obligations

Child/infant care and care of other dependants

The question regarding infant care concerns 40% of the sample with the majority saying that this care is shared among more than one person (26.6%).

Infant care		N	%	Valid %
Valid	Mother	15	5.5	6.0
	Grandparent	11	4.0	4.4
	House maid	1	.4	0.4
	Nursery schools	7	2.6	2.8
	Other person	2	0.7	0.8
	Many people	66	24.3	26.6
	Does not concern me	146	53.7	58.9
	Total	248	91.2	100.0
Void	.	24	8.8	
Total		272	100.0	

Of those who said the care is undertaken by one person, 60% say it is the mother, while the father takes just over half the percentage of the mother (34%). The grandparents undertake the care of infants in most cases (48%) compared to the father (34%).

Summary Table A

	Mother %	Father %	Grandparent %	House maid %	Nursery schools %	Only one person %	N
Infant care	60	34	48	8	22	35	102
Child care after school	42	29	31	10	4	51	186
Care of elderly parents	30	25	2	10		20	83
Transport of children to school	41	40	11			38	182
Transport of children to private lessons	48	44	16			50	160
Homework	51	45	10			49	172

Thoughts and Notes on the Issues of Reconciliation
of Work and Family Life in Europe.

91

A similar situation exists with the care of children after school. This care concerns 79% of those who answered.

Child care after school		N	%	Valid %
Valid	Mother	42	15.4	17.9
	Father	5	1.8	2.1
	Grandparent	35	12.9	14.9
	House maid	4	1.5	1.7
	Nursery schools	4	1.5	1.7
	Other person	5	1.8	2.1
	Many persons	90	33.1	38.3
	Does not concern me	50	18.4	21.3
	Total	235	86.4	100.0
Void	.	37	13.6	
Total		272	100.0	

However, from those who said one person is responsible for the care of children after school, the hierarchy, beginning from the largest percentage, is as follows: the mother (18%), a grandparent (15%) and the father (2%). The largest group of those asked say that this care is undertaken by many persons (38%). Among these, the hierarchy of care is repeated with one of the persons being the mother (42%), a grandparent (31%) and finally the father (29%) (See Summary Table A).

Regarding the care of elderly parents, only 31% of those asked responded to this question. Of those who responded and said that only one person was responsible, it was the mother again that had the greatest responsibility (25%), followed by the elderly parents who take care of themselves (23%) and the house maid (12%). In cases where the responsibility is shared among many persons, it is again the mother that has the greatest responsibility (30%), along with the father (25%) and the house maid (10%).

Care of elderly parents		N	%	Valid %
Valid	Mother	21	7.7	25.0
	Father	3	1.1	3.6
	Grandparent	19	7.0	22.6
	House maid	10	3.7	11.9
	Other person	2	0.7	2.4
	Many persons	28	10.3	33.3
	Does not concern me	1	0.4	1.2
	Total	84	30.9	100.0
Void	.	188	69.1	
Total		272	100.0	

The transportation of children to school is shared almost equally between the two parents. When only one person transports the children, it is 21% the mother and 17% the father. Most (35%) share the responsibility, with the mother (41%) and the father (40%) having a similar participation. A similar image appears regarding the proportion of responsibility for their transportation to private lessons.

Transportation of children to school		N	%	Valid %
Valid	Mother	47	17.3	20.8
	Father	38	14.0	16.8
	Grandparent	10	3.7	4.4
	Nursery schools	1	.4	.4
	Other person	8	2.9	3.5
	Many persons	78	28.7	34.5
	Does not concern me	44	16.2	19.5
	Total	226	83.1	100.0
Void	.	46	16.9	
Total		272	100.0	

Thoughts and Notes on the Issues of Reconciliation
of Work and Family Life in Europe.

93

When only one person is responsible, the mother (19%) has almost double the responsibility than the father (10.8%). When this responsibility is shared by more than one person (35%), the parents have the main and almost equal responsibility (mother 48%, father 44%).

Transportation of children to private lessons		N	%	Valid %
Valid	Mother	44	16.2	19.0
	Father	25	9.2	10.8
	Grandparent	6	2.2	2.6
	Other person	5	1.8	2.2
	Many persons	81	29.8	34.9
	Does not concern me	71	26.1	30.6
	Total	232	85.3	100.0
Void	.	40	14.7	
Total		272	100.0	

Regarding the children's homework, the mother has a much higher responsibility both when she says she is the main person responsible (28%) as when she shares the responsibility with the father (51%, see Summary Table A).

Homework		N	%	Valid %
Valid	Mother	65	23.9	27.5
	Father	11	4.0	4.7
	Grandparent	3	1.1	1.3
	Other person	5	1.8	2.1
	Many persons	88	32.4	37.3
	Does not concern me	64	23.5	27.1
	Total	236	86.8	100.0
Void	.	36	13.2	
Total		272	100.0	

Childcare, apart from parents, after school

Apart from the parents, childcare beyond school hours is undertaken to a great extent (67%) by the grandparents. This hyper-dependency on an informal form of care is a special characteristic of the Cypriot society. This explains why the childcare system of workers has not collapsed despite the absence of public and private forms of care after school hours. The implementation of the all-day school has been applied only to a restricted number of primary schools. Even in these cases, the afternoon occupation of the children does not cover the working hours of most parents in the private sector.

Who usually takes care of your children after school hours, apart from you or your current partner?	%
Grandparents	67%
Ex-spouse/partner	1
Another member of the family	4
Another form of free care, care by someone here or at their own house	4
Paid care, care by someone here or at there house	0.5
Free child station or care outside the house	2
Child station or paid care outside the house	8
The child stays home alone	10
It does not need care from outside (I do not work outside the home, there is always a parent at home)	1

N=218

Persons responsible for other family obligations

As we see from the results presented in the following Summary Table B, there is a common picture for all the responsibilities included in the table.

Thoughts and Notes on the Issues of Reconciliation
of Work and Family Life in Europe.

95

Summary Table B

Responsibilities	Only one person %						Many persons %				
	Mother	Father	Grandparent	Many persons	Does not concern me	N	Mother	Father	Grandparent	House maid	N
Medical care of elderly parents	23	10	18	44		125	41	36	10	6	125
Medical care of children/infants	23	4	1	57	16	248	67	60	17	2	209
Communication with teachers	38	6	0.4	36	20	240	45	44	2		192
Child care on school holidays	12	3	15	48	19	229	57	52	20	5	88
Shopping for children's needs	48	1		34	16	256	41	39	8	1	213
Mobility/ entertainment of elderly parents	22	8	18	49		122	48	45	5	4	122
Entertainment of children/ infants	13	3		68	16	250	80	78	25	3	209

Among those asked who said one person is responsible, the mother always has the primary role with a great difference compared to the father and the rest of the persons. One exception is the childcare during school holidays, when the grandparents (15%) have a very small lead compared to the mother (12%). The large differences in undertaking duties by women and men are evident in a very characteristic manner in communication with teachers, where 38% of women take on the role, compared to only 6% of men. The same huge differences appear in shopping for children's needs with almost 50% of women doing it compared to 1% of men.

When there are many persons undertaking the responsibilities, the differences between men and women are reduced significantly, however with the mother leading compared to the father in all cases.

3.4. Men-women work time

Time for housework

The average time allocated for housework by all members of the household is four hours daily. Housework includes cooking, washing up, cleaning, clothes care, shopping, property maintenance, but not child care and leisure activities. Personal time is divided as follows:

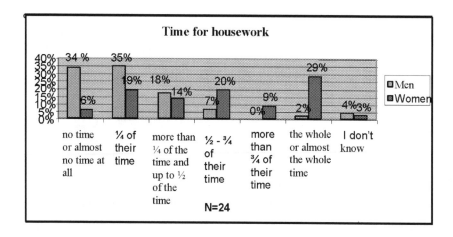

The differences between men and women are significant and show the unequal distribution of housework. The scale for measuring work time is between "no time at all" and "the whole of the time". As the work time at home is reduced, the percentage of men in this category increases. On the contrary, as the work time increases, so does the percentage of women. Specifically, 34% of men compared to only 6% of women spend "no time or almost no time at all". On the other hand of the scale, 29% of women compared to 2% of men spend "the whole or almost the whole time". The differences are reduced somewhat only in the category "more than ¼ of the time and up to half the time" with 18% of men compared to 14% of women. This situation is also verified when those asked are called on to measure the time from their total time that their spouse/partner dedicates to housework.

Thoughts and Notes on the Issues of Reconciliation
of Work and Family Life in Europe.

97

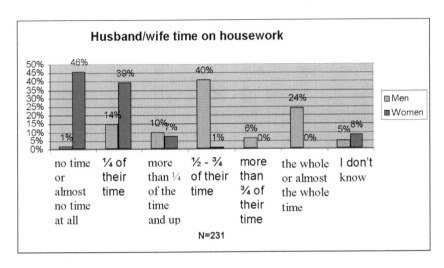

Among women, 46% say that their husband does not spend any time, while only 1% of men said the same about their wives. The image is reversed on the other end of the scale, where 24% of men say their wife spends "the whole or almost the whole of her time", while no woman said the same about her husband (0%). There are also big differences when the working time exceeds half to ¾ of the total working time. The largest percentage in men (41%) believe their wives spend more than half their time, while among women it is almost zero (0.7%).

Time for other family obligations

Apart from the housework, those asked counted the monthly hours they allocate to the following family obligations:

Obligations	N	Minimum	Maximum	Average
Bank transactions	217	0	30	3.05
Medical coverage	173	0	30	2.75
Insurance coverage	111	0	10	1.05
Family budget	169	0	60	4.21
Obligations with the public sector	164	0	20	1.95

The average monthly time for each obligation, such as bank transactions, medical coverage, insurance coverage, family budget and obligations with the public sector does not exceed four hours per month. As we mentioned above, the average daily time for housework is four hours, with women spending more time on it than men.

Working time

Regarding the working time, there do not seem to be significant differences between men and women. A fourth of the sample works with the somewhat "privileged" timetable of 6am-7am to 2pm-2.30pm, which mainly covers the public and semi-governmental sectors, local administration and banks. This timetable is considered to be "privileged" because it reduces to the minimum the time of absence of parents from their children after school hours.

	Timetable	N	%	Valid %
Valid	6:00-7:00 to 14:00-14:30	67	24.6	24.8
	7:00 to 15:00-16:00	45	16.5	16.7
	7:30-8:00 to 17:00-19:00	32	11.8	11.9
	8:00 to 14:00-14:30	27	9.9	10.0
	8:00-9:00 to 16:00-17:00	26	9.6	9.6
	8:00-9:00 to 20:00-21:00	7	2.6	2.6
	8:00-9:00 to 18:00-19:00	19	7.0	7.0
	Afternoon work	5	1.8	1.9
	Morning/Afternoon work	27	9.9	10.0
	Flexible timetable	12	4.4	4.4
	Part-time employment	1	0.4	0.4
	Other	2	0.7	0.7
	Total	270	99.3	100.0

Thoughts and Notes on the Issues of Reconciliation
of Work and Family Life in Europe.

99

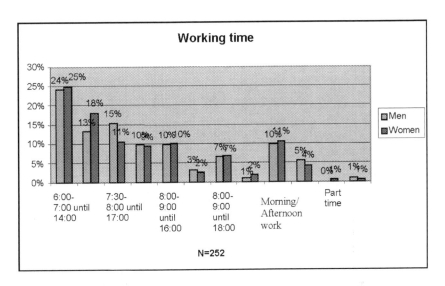

Overtime

The average of weekly overtime is 8 hours with 40% of the sample saying they work overtime.

Do you work overtime?		N	%	Valid %
Valid	Yes	102	37.5	39.7
	No	155	57.0	60.3
	Total	257	94.5	100.0

Out of those who work overtime, 82% work in the private sector and 15% in the public or semi-governmental sector of local administration. This comparatively low participation of the public sector in overtime improves the already "privileged" timetable of the workers in this sector. This is in relation to the time outside work, which remains and can theoretically be dedicated to the needs of the family.

Sector	Do you work overtime?					
	Yes		No		Total	
	N	%	N	%	N	%
Public, semi-governmental, local administration	15	14.7%	56	36.6%	71	27.8%
Private	84	82.4%	93	60.8%	177	69.4%
Other	3	2.9%	4	2.6%	7	2.7%
Total	102	100.0%	153	100.0%	255	100.0%

A larger percentage of men (48%) seems to work the most overtime compared to the percentage among women (35%).

Do you work overtime?	Men		Women		Total	
	N	%	N	%	N	%
Yes	42	47.7%	53	34.6%	95	39.4%
No	46	52.3%	100	65.4%	146	60.6%
Total	88	100.0%	153	100.0%	241	100.0%

Time for professional activities

The average for vocational training is 12 days per year, for seminars 9, for professional trips 7 and for leave for family reasons 15 days.

	N	Minimum	Maximum	Average
Vocational training	153	0	150	11.86
Seminars	152	0	50	9.08
Professional trips	94	0	90	7.49
Leave for family reasons	208	0	30	14.00

Thoughts and Notes on the Issues of Reconciliation
of Work and Family Life in Europe.

101

Personal-family income

The gender form of employment we described in Unit 1 with the horizontal and vertical professional division, is verified with the layering of income.

Annual gross personal income	Men		Women		Total	
	N	%	N	%	N	
Up to 7,000	6	6.7%	58	36.0%	64	25.5%
7,001-15,000	45	50.0%	78	48.4%	123	49.0%
15,0001-20,000	19	21.1%	17	10.6%	36	14.3%
Over 20,000	20	22.2%	8	5.0%	28	11.2%
Total	90	100.0%	161	100.0%	251	100.0%

Even though in the middle category with an annual gross personal income of £7001-£15,000, men (50%) and women (49%) have a similar representation, the differences are intense in the extreme categories. Among men, only 7% are in the lowest income category with an annual gross personal income of up to £7000, while in women this percentage reaches 36%. On the contrary, in the high income category with an income of over £20,000, one finds 22% of men compared to 5% of women.

When the personal income is half or less than the total income, the percentage among women is higher than that among men. When the income is over half, the roles are reversed. Only 9% of women compared to 21% of men has an income that constitutes a "very high" percentage of the total income of the household.

What percentage does your personal income represent in the total income of your household?	Men		Women		Total	
	N	%	N	%	N	%
Zero	0	0%	3	2.0%	3	1.3%
Very small	3	3.4%	9	5.9%	12	5.0%
Under half	4	4.6%	32	20.9%	36	15.0%
About half	21	24.1%	58	37.9%	79	32.9%
Over half	24	27.6%	17	11.1%	41	17.1%
Very high	18	20.7%	14	9.2%	32	13.3%
The whole percentage	14	16.1%	17	11.1%	31	12.9%
I will not answer	3	3.4%	2	1.3%	5	2.1%
I do not know	0	0%	1	0.7%	1	.4%
Total	87	100.0%	153	100.0%	240	100.0%

3.5. Stances in relation to the "family-professional obligation dilemma"

In this unit, the sample was asked to say to what degree they agree or disagree with a number of statements, which will be indicative of their stances and the differences between the genders in relation to the "family-professional obligation dilemma".

Time for childcare and self

Men and women of the sample react differently to the first two statements if the time they spend on childcare and themselves is satisfactory. Men seem to be more satisfied compared to women about the time they have at their disposal both for the children and themselves. Specifically, as we see in the following graph, almost half the men (49.4%) say they agree with the statement about children, compared to 37% of women. On the other hand, only about a quarter of men (26.5%) disagrees compared to 39% of women. The same situation exists regarding available time for the self. A quarter of women seem to disagree to a great extent with

Thoughts and Notes on the Issues of Reconciliation
of Work and Family Life in Europe.

103

the statement that they have time for themselves, while only 11% of men feel the same.

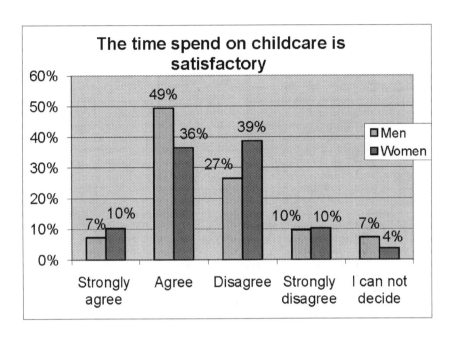

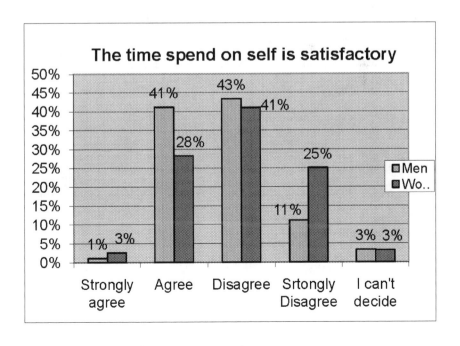

Distribution of family responsibilities

The differences in the perceptions of men and women are much more significant regarding the statement that the distribution of family responsibilities is fair. On the whole, men are much more positive, with 68% agreeing and agreeing intensely, compared to 38% of a positive stance by women. The majority of women (54%) do not agree with the statement compared to 24% of men. From these stances the great difference of views and notions of the two genders is apparent regarding the multiple responsibilities of the family. Basically, for a large percentage of men, multiple family responsibilities are considered to be a "fair" privilege of women.

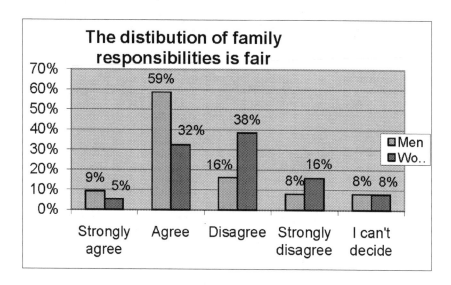

Influence of family and professional responsibilities

The views of those asked are divided around the issue of stress and fatigue regarding family and professional responsibilities transferred from the house to the workplace and vice versa. There are no significant gender differences.

Thoughts and Notes on the Issues of Reconciliation
of Work and Family Life in Europe.

105

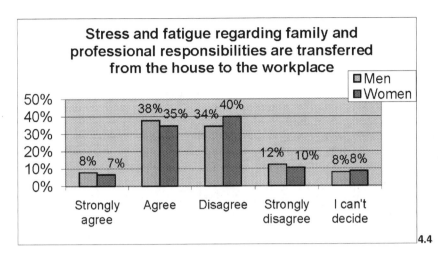

4.4

Women, family and work

To the statement if a woman should be prepared to abandon her job for the sake of her family, the women disagree more intensely (25%) than the men (13%). However, the majority of both genders react negatively to the statement, with 64% of women and 56% of men.

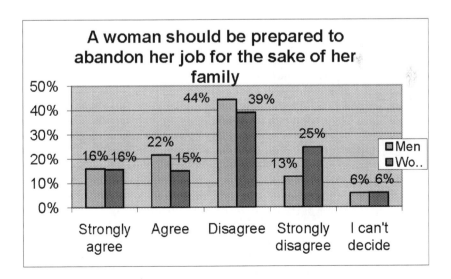

Both spouses appear tolerant regarding the pressure of work, with more than half of the men and women disagreeing with the statement.

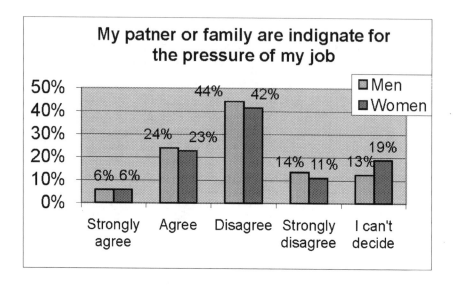

Importance of criteria in choosing a job

The overwhelming majority considers important all the criteria in choosing a job, such as: security, high income, good prospects for advancement, taking initiative and the possibility of combining professional-family life (See the five following tables in detail). The only difference between men and women is the degree of importance they give to the criteria. Men consider them more important compared to women, who just consider them important.

Thoughts and Notes on the Issues of Reconciliation
of Work and Family Life in Europe.

107

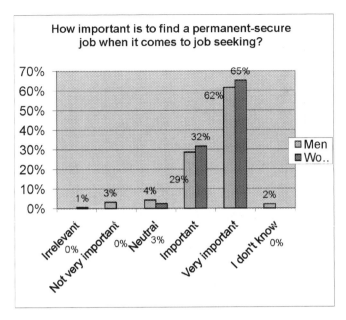

N=249

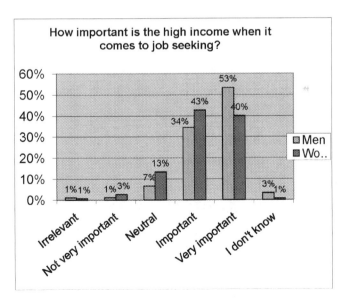

N=247

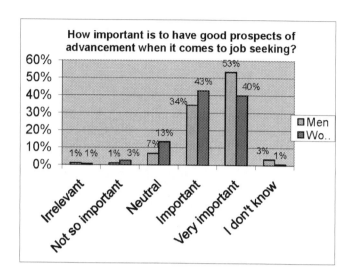

N=240

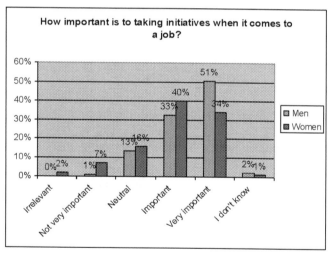

N=245

Thoughts and Notes on the Issues of Reconciliation
of Work and Family Life in Europe.

109

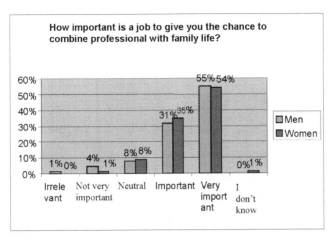

N=244

Preferred working time

The workers of the sample were asked about the working time they would like to work, having in mind that the remuneration would be proportional to the working hours. The average on working time is 36 hours per week with values fluctuating between 20 to 72 hours (N=232).

Total time at home for full-time care of children

Those asked were requested to calculate the total time they spend at home for the full-time care of their children, including maternity leave or parental leave. The answers are indicative and are directly linked to the legal measures existing in this sector. The highest percentage of women (52%) says it dedicated 6 months, that is not more time than the legislation provides for regarding maternity leave. With the absence of a measure for paid paternity leave, the large majority does not dedicate time to the children. Recent parental leave, as long as it is unpaid, has not yet been used much by working parents.

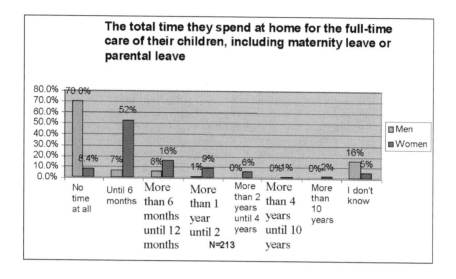

For those who have dedicated time for the full-time care of their children, the majority believes their career has not been affected negatively.

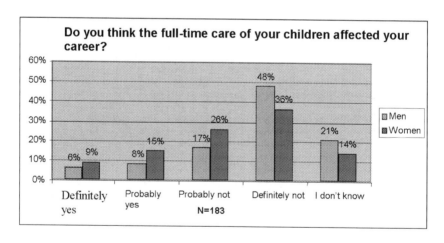

3.6. *Views regarding the introduction of "equality strategies"*

The purpose of the last unit was to chart the views of the workers regarding the introduction of "Equality Strategies" in businesses. These strategies were interpreted as measures through which working environments that are women-friendly would be created, e.g. with the

Thoughts and Notes on the Issues of Reconciliation
of Work and Family Life in Europe.

111

implementation of flexible timetables and flexible forms of employment, provision of child care stations (See Bibliography Review and the case of Interorient company) and Equality Advisors. Those asked were requested to agree or disagree with a number of statements concerning the hypothetical introduction of "Equality Strategies" in businesses. The reactions in general were very positive for all four measures presented.

Usefulness of measures

Regarding the first statement, if such measures would be necessary and useful, the only difference between men and women was the degree of agreement, with women agreeing more intensely (45%) with the statement than men (28%).

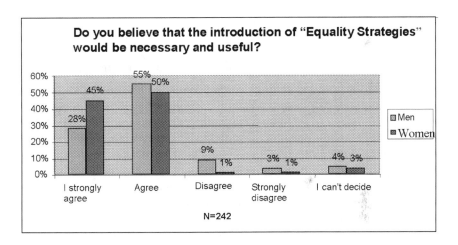

Professional progress and competitiveness

In the reactions regarding the statement if the measures would help professional progress and competitiveness, it appears to be a differentiation of views among the two genders. Among women, 78% agree or agree intensely, while only half of the men are positive. A fourth of the men disagree with the statement, while in women the percentage is only 10%.

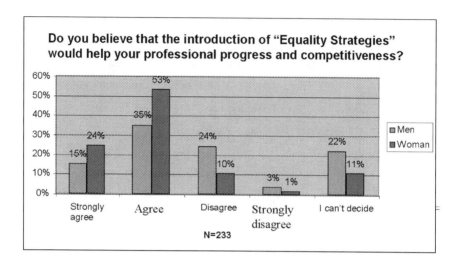

Influence of Equality Strategies on the family and professional life

Even though the majority of both genders agree with both statements regarding the influence of Equality Strategies on the family and professional life, the percentage of positive answers among women is higher than that of men. In total, 67% of men have a positive stance to the statement that it will improve the quality of family life, compared to 87% of women.

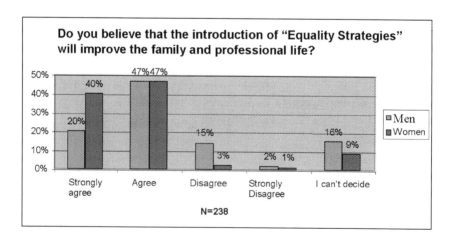

Thoughts and Notes on the Issues of Reconciliation
of Work and Family Life in Europe.

113

The difference among the two genders remains similar to the statement regarding the improvement of the quality of working conditions as the result of the future introduction of Equality Strategies.

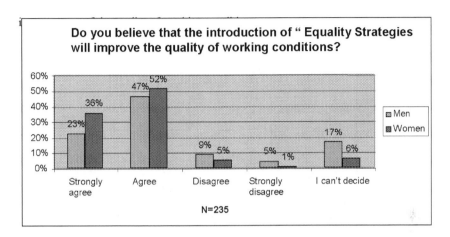

Do you believe that the introduction of " Equality Strategies will improve the quality of working conditions?

N=235

3.7. Summary of main findings

The main findings of the quantitative study are summarized as follows:

- **Gender form of employment** with a horizontal and vertical division in professional categories (37.5% of women are "secretaries, cashiers" compared to 4.4% of men. 27.5% of men hold managerial positions compared to 8.8% of women).

- When **infant care** is undertaken by more than one person, 60% state the mother, 48% a grandparent and 34% the father.

- **Child care after school hours**
  o When one person is responsible for childcare after school hours, the hierarchy of care is: the mother (18%), a grandparent (15%) and the father (2%).
  o When the care is undertaken by many persons (38%): the mother (42%), a grandparent (31%) and the father (29%).

- **Care of elderly parents**
  - o When only one person is responsible, the mother has the highest responsibility (25%), both elderly parents (23%) and the house maid (12%).
  - o When the responsibility is shared, the mother has the largest responsibility (30%), along with the father (25%) and the house maid (10%).

- The **transportation of children to school** and to private lessons is shared almost equally between both parents.

- The mother has a much higher responsibility for **the children's homework** both when she is stated as the main person responsible (28%) and when she shares the responsibility with the father (51%).

- Apart from the parents, the **childcare after school** is undertaken to a great extent (67%) by a grandparent.

- **Persons responsible for the medical care, communication, shopping, transportation and entertainment**
  - o When one persons is responsible, the mother always has the primary role with a great difference:
    - ▪ In communication with teachers the mother undertakes the role by 38% and the father by 6%.
    - ▪ In shopping for children's needs: 50% of women compared to only 1% of men.
  - o When there are many persons, the differences between men and women are reduced significantly with the mother, however, leading compared to the father in all cases.

- There are significant differences between men and women in **sharing housework**
  - o 34% of men compared to only 6% of women spend "no time or almost no time"

Thoughts and Notes on the Issues of Reconciliation
of Work and Family Life in Europe.

115

- o   29% of women compared to 2% of men spend "all their time or almost all their time"

- **Layering of income**: There are intense differences in extreme categories: only 7% of men are in the lowest income category with an income of up to £7000, compared to 36% of women. In the highest income category (>£20,000), 22% of men, compared to 5% of women.

- Perceptions regarding the family-professional obligation dilemma
  - o   Men are more satisfied regarding the time they spend on their children and themselves: 49.4% of men agree with the statement on children, compared to 37% of women. A quarter of women disagree intensely that they have time for themselves, while 11% feel the same.
  - o   Men are much more positive: 68% agree intensely that the distribution of family responsibilities is fair, compared to 38% of women. 54% of women do not agree, compared to 24% of men.
  - o   Views are divided regarding the statement that stress and fatigue concerning family and professional responsibilities are transferred from home to the workplace and vice versa. There do not appear to be significant gender differences.
  - o   To the statement if a woman should be prepared to leave her job for the sake of her family, women agreed more intensely (25%) than men (13%). The majority of both genders reacts negatively, with 64% of women and 56% of men.

- The overwhelming majority considers all the criteria in choosing a job to be important, such as security, high income, and good prospects for progress, taking initiatives and the possibility of combining professional-family life.

- 52% of women dedicated up to 6 months for the full-time care of their children, including maternity or parental leave.

- Differentiation of views between the two genders on the influence of measures for the introduction of "Equality Strategies" on professional progress and competitiveness: 78% of women agree or agree intensely, while just half the men are positive. A quarter of the men disagree with the statement, compared to 10% of women.

- The majority of both genders agree with the positive influence of Equality Strategies on the family and professional life: 67% of men maintain a positive stance to the statement that it will improve the quality of family life, compared to 87% of women.

3.8 *Proposed measures*

Cyprus has already conformed its family law with the European data since 1995 (L. 19(1)1995), especially as far as children's protection is concerned, although it was not a member of the European Union then. In 2003 law L.104(1)2003 modernized the institution of marriage by the establishment of the civil wedding among Greek-Cypriot citizens as well as among Greek-Cypriot citizens and others. A very significant aspect of this law is the fact that civil weddings between Greek-Cypriot and Turkish-Cypriot citizens are allowed for the first time (Gasouka, 2007). During the procedure of adjustment to the European acquis, Cyprus also proceeded to the adjustment of legislation relevant to maternity, which concerns laws related to parenthood and parental leaves, maternity protection (maternity leave, prohibition of dismissal of pregnant women, facilitation of breast-feeding), protection and care of childhood, creation of a family court etc. Of special interest is the institution of family mediation that concerns every family affair including parental care, children's maintenance and property relations between husband and wife etc. that complies with Recommendation R98 of the Council of the Ministers to the member-states. In Cyprus the actions concerning issues such as protection of motherhood, family and

Thoughts and Notes on the Issues of Reconciliation
of Work and Family Life in Europe.

117

childhood protection, combating domestic violence etc., the treatment of which is a precondition of the reconciliation of family and professional life, are still under the jurisdiction of the National Mechanism for Women's Rights and several other equality institutions, NGOs etc.

From the overall effort – but for some occasional exceptions thanks to the Cyprus Employers and Industrialists Federation – the employers and especially the Cypriot businesses were missing, which do not yet systematically include gender dimension in their corporate environment and their business options, although most of them have a very powerful social profile. At the same time a powerful non-conformity is quite evident between the institutional framework [9] and the social practice, as the patriarchal traditional perceptions on the social roles of gender demonstrate significant historical endurance and unwillingness to differentiate, despite the formal public rhetoric which is relevant to gender equality and equal opportunities. However, nowadays the recognition of the significance that the promotion of gender equality with emphasis on the reconciliation of the employees' – and especially the women's – family and professional life has for the economic growth and the social cohesion of the Cypriot society is common ground. One must not however forget that in the framework of interprofessional dialogue the European social partners are committed during the Spring Summit in March 2005 to a "Framework of Actions for the promotion of gender equality" with an implementation and consequences calculation deadline in 2008 (KETHI, 2007) and Cyprus, although recently a full E.U. member, will have to present its relevant national experience soon, in order to contribute to the design and dissemination of "proper practices and actions at national, sectoral, local and business level" (KETHI, 2007). At the same time, although the biggest part of the responsibility belongs to the State, the fact that the issue of gender equality more generally and reconciliation more specifically directly concerns both the employers and civil society, men and women, something that calls for direct changes in the collective social consciousness and the set of attitudes and beliefs related to gender, is common ground. This particular study, drawing from both the Cypriot reality and the now rich European experience and the multitude of positive practices that emerge from it, results in a package of proposals that can be utilized by the State and the Cypriot social-economic institutions, which, although indicative, it is possible to direct future institutional actions. More specifically:

I. To the State:

- Immediate integration of the gender dimension in the educational procedure of the pre-school, primary, secondary and vocational (initial and continuing) education with a relevant adjustment of the curriculum, the school textbooks and simultaneous training/sensitisation of the teachers on issues of gender equality and equal opportunities.

- Immediate integration of Gender Studies in all Universities and all their Departments.

- Training/sensitisation of the Ministry officials – and especially of the Ministry of Education, the Ministry of Economics and the Ministry of Employment – for the integration of gender dimension in all policies and the possibility to evaluate consequences. More specifically, preparation of the Ministry of Economics officials in order to become capable of Gender Budgeting.

- Financing of research and studies by Universities and other institutions for the registration of gender inequalities in the Cypriot labour market, their causes and their qualities as well as specialized proposals for their elimination.

-Legal clarification of an expanded definition of modern "family", without prejudice and exclusions, which will include the equity of its members and will contribute to the reconciliation/co-ordination of their family and professional life (Pilavaki, 2007)

- Adoption of direct measures of protection and support of "sensitive" families (single-parent families, families with dependent members, large families etc.)

Thoughts and Notes on the Issues of Reconciliation
of Work and Family Life in Europe.

119

- Legislative protection of extended, fully paid paternity leave (Pilavaki, 2007)

- Reform of the inflexible rules of working time regulation.

- Synchronisation of societal hours (city hours) and working hours [10].

- Regulation of insurance and pension rights and encouragement of men to make use of parental leave.

- Establishment of new childcare structures and improvement of the quality and accessibility of the already existing ones, with free provision of care, or – in the worst case – with services at so low prices in order to be affordable to the economically weak groups of the population [11].

- Establishment of permanent or occasional dependent persons care provision structures, in combination to various caretakers' reinforcement measures.

- Financing from national and E.U. resources of businesses of every size in Cyprus for the development of actions such as the establishment of day-care nurseries in their facilities, training of female employees in new professional subjects or the sensitisation of men with regard to reconciliation, the emergence of the paternal role, etc.

- Regulation of organisations', services', public and private businesses' professional working hours and legislative regulation of the correspondence of the working hours of the public and private services (i.e. a civil service employing parents and a private day-care nursery)[12].

- Provision of economic or tax incentives to public or private businesses and institutions in order to promote gender equality and reconciliation of family and professional life for their employees through defined actions ("balanced employment of men and women in empty or new positions, women's promotion to managerial positions, adoption of innovative programs of working hours management, so that men and women could be facilitated in their family obligations etc. after the certification of implementation of relevant plans" (KETHI, 2007).

- Adoption of incentives similar to the above that will contribute to changing gender-related stereotypes, highlight the new domestic and public roles of the sexes, emphasise on the importance of a new fatherhood for children and family and promote through their programmes and commercials the connection of economy, social inclusion and democracy with equality and the reconciliation of family and professional life.

- Establishment of annual awards to businesses, organisations and the Media.

- Development of employment policies aiming at informing the social partners and the businesses about the cost and the benefits resulting from Reconciliation processes that integrate the gender dimension.

- Development of a recurrent campaign of sensitisation and informing the public opinion about the content and the philosophy of the importance of gender equality and equal opportunities, with an emphasis on the big social demand for Reconciliation. These campaigns should raise the fundamental issue of the redistribution of the social roles of the sexes inside the family, the redistribution of family time in favour of women as well and the replacement of biological with social motherhood (Gasouka, 2008).

- Establishment of Structures for counseling women on employment, entrepreneurship and networking, some of which being mobile.

- Establishment of an Observatory for the Reconciliation of Family and professional Life, that is a documentation centre, aiming at the collection, processing and utilisation of qualitative and quantitative data related to that significant social demand in Cyprus, with a simultaneous dissemination of relevant information and positive practices and examples as well as the creation (design-realisation) and submission or similar research, studies and proposals to the State or anyone interested, with simultaneous development of networks of business relations to social-economic institutions and public services both at national and international level (Gasouka, 2008)

Thoughts and Notes on the Issues of Reconciliation
of Work and Family Life in Europe.

121

From all the above-mentioned, the fundamental role of the State to the accomplishment of Gender Equality and Equal Opportunities and especially Reconciliation is evident. For this study this role is the most important, while the roles of the social institutions and the civil society are exceptionally important but always complementary and auxiliary. And as the State shoulders this big social, economic and political responsibility, it also has to provide the necessary financial resources for its realisation. Without realising the significance that gender dimension of economical state budgets has nowadays – something that has been recently put forward by the E.U. bodies – it would be an illusion to expect radical changes both in the field of labour and family, and society in general.

II. To the businesses

- Design of business strategies of Reconciliation of professional and family life of the employees and especially of the women with gender dimension (Reconciliation plans).

- Improvement and enrichment of family friendly policies, where they already exist.

- Encouragement and promotion of radical changes in labour organisation and business mentality.

- Implementation of measures for the improvement of the possibility of employing persons with family obligations and for the quality of balance between work and family obligations.

- Incorporation of the reconciliation of family and labour dimension in the collective negotiations' agenda.

- Establishment of childcare structures in the facilities of medium and large businesses or financing the parents for this reason.

- Establishment of a new type of work position and a new professional profile, that of the Equality Advisor with the responsibility of designing and realising actions concerning Equal Opportunities and Reconciliation.

- Organisation of seminars and conferences concerning the information/ sensitisation of officials and employees on the significance of the Reconciliation of family and professional life of the employees and especially of the women and the utilisation of their lost skills, talents, expectations and wishes.

- Development of corporativeness and networking actions with social-economic institutions among which are trade unions and Equality institutions.

Along with the businesses in the specific sector it is necessary for the employing organisations to take certain actions, such as:

- Conduct of research on gender discriminations in the labour market and studies on the contribution of the businesses to their elimination.

- Initiatives of relevant information/sensitisation of their members on the institutional framework, the incentives and the positive European practices.

- Actions of enforcement of women's entrepreneurship and their promotion to managerial positions.

- Design of models of new types of work organisation, which take family needs into account.

III. To trade unions

The role of trade unions to the achievement of eliminating gender discrimination and the realisation of gender equality is of utmost importance. We should never forget that it often acts as the voice of female (and male) employees in expressing and asserting their occupational demands. As mentioned, (KETHI, 2007) "trade unions must actively participate in the promotion of regulations for the harmonisation of family and professional life, promote systematic measures of preventing gender or social discrimination or loss of protection, pointing out

Thoughts and Notes on the Issues of Reconciliation
of Work and Family Life in Europe.

123

workers' relevant needs at the same time. Trade unions should intensify their efforts in promoting measures of education and training that will help working parents respond more effectively to the balancing of family and professional life". However, the following should be added to these:

- information/sensitisation of their members regarding the demand of gender equality in all areas of the social, economic and political life.

- Design of policies in order to highlight female executives in their frame and election of a significant number of women in their bodies.

- Adaptation of their modus operandi and their discourses to women's needs and life style, in order to render trade unions more appealing to women.

- Ensuring women's participation at all levels of collective negotiations.

- Firmness in defending full-time employment, as a dominant employment model for men and women (KETHI, 2007).

- Establishment of as many as possible childcare structures, so that parents and especially mothers can exercise their trade union activities without obstacles.

- Integration of the gender dimension in all training activities of the trade unions and their scientific-training structures.

Integration of the gender dimension in collective labour agreements and all the agreements included in the Collective Labour Agreements at all levels.

IV. To the Civil Society

It is obvious that the Civil Society and its institutions – above all women's organisations and equality institutions – act as pressure groups, but also contribution to the State towards achieving Equality and especially the Reconciliation. It is necessary that they actively participate in the design and development of all processes and regulations, especially those that reinforce the family and professional balance, but also women's human/social rights that are questioned even today under the pressure of the patriarchal commands. They should aim for dialogue, the exchange of positive and negative experiences, the dissemination of information, and if this is not possible, fight for it. They should promote networking with each other, and endorse the development of forms of cooperativeness and networking with employing, scientific, academic and other institutions, but also with institutions of the broader public sector, aiming at establishing measures and policies that promote gender equality and equal opportunities and especially the balancing of professional and family life of working people and – the emphasis is not accidental – especially women, that are still burdened by the multiple roles of the private sphere of life and their occupation.

In light of the things mentioned above, it is advisable that there will be a formulation of a series of actions aiming at raising the difficulties in achieving a reconciliation/harmonisation of family and professional life and creating opportune conditions for the implementation of measures and actions to the advantage of this important issue, through the production of knowledge regarding the parameters of the problem.[13] Among the first relevant actions, the establishment of an Observatory seems particularly useful – an Observatory that includes a set of actions aiming at a multidimensional intervention, both for recording the phenomenon and monitoring its progress, and for formulating and implementing coherent suggestions/proposals for policy planning and taking initiatives based on gender perspective.

What is an observatory

It is a structure equipped with the relevant human resources and the necessary logistical infrastructure that operates – at least in Cyprus – in the framework of two ministries responsible for gender issues, the Ministry of Justice and the Ministry of Labour. It systematically combines economotechnical, scientific, research, informational and administrative activity, with the organised cooperation and cooperativeness in national

Thoughts and Notes on the Issues of Reconciliation
of Work and Family Life in Europe.

125

and international level. It aims at producing/offering social services and scientific knowledge and it has the necessary means and tools to achieve its goals and aspirations. It stands out for its financial and administrative autonomy, and its legal entrenchment. In its practice and operation it constitutes a system, that is a harmonically organised set, comprised of the abovementioned elements, which are interdependent in the realisation of its goals and objectives (Holevas, 1995). The inputs and outputs of the structure are the expression of these elements. Inputs are the necessary human and material resources as well as information of any nature that come in to be utilized. Outputs are the transformations of resources into products/services based on a particular organisational process.

The aim of the operation of an Observatory is *the assumption of a primary role in the collection of data and statistics regarding important social issues/demands of our time, by which it can later feed the relevant policies and practices of the State and widely social, economical, gender, etc. agencies.* Based on this quality, the Observatory cooperates with governmental or non-governmental, national or international organisations, responsible for relevant issues (e.g. phenomena of racism or xenophobia, unemployment, violence against women, children's rights, etc.). The Observatory coordinates its activities with the corresponding actions of the national government and the institutions of the E.U. It should be noted however that the information forwarded to the Observatory can only be used for the abovementioned purposes and under the conditions set by the forwarding service. Their level of protection will be equivalent to the one that arises from the orders of Directive 95/46/EC. On the other hand, public organisations are not obliged to provide information characterised as confidential in their national law.

As an institution the Observatory was highlighted by the E.U., which recognises the importance of cooperation for combating the abovementioned social problems, the added value of information from other people's experiences and the importance of collecting objective and reliable data through the utilisation of New Technologies and not only those. Besides these particular problems constitute clear violations of human dignity, human rights and the fundamental freedoms on which the European Union is based. By the institution of the Observatories that the Community promotes it confirms (as several national governments of course) that the policies and practices introduced are most appropriate and best targeted. In short, the Observatory is a critical weapon in the arsenal of combating social discrimination and inequality and, especially in this case, the one which is connected to gender (Diamantopoulou, 2007). Given the contemporary circumstances its imperativeness is undisputed and its role appears to be exceptionally important. Thanks to the operation of various Observatories to this day we are in a position to form a clearer picture about issues such as racism, trafficking, or any kind of violation of human rights, etc. For example it appears that the role of the European Monitoring Centre (EUMC) [14] is quite important in international level in the field of racism and discrimination in the E.U., as well as that of everyday situation of ethnic minorities. In its latest annual report it focused in the field of employment and access to education, as well as housing for the first time (Diamantopoulou, 2007). Its operation proved that the production of comparable data regarding what happens in every country allows for successful practices to be detected, practices that can be implemented (with the proper encouragement) in other countries that need them. It is evident therefore that the collection, analysis and the appropriate dissemination of data are the added value of EUMC. Of course of equal importance and breadth are the Observatory for Employment in Dublin and the Observatories of Equal Opportunities [15] and Women's Health [16] that take action in Spain, etc. From the point of organisational structure and operation special interest is showed by the Observatory constituted in Greece by the "Information Society", a company of the Greek public sector to which the present study owes a lot.

An Observatory should, apart from the collection, analysis and dissemination of data, take action in the design and realisation of

Thoughts and Notes on the Issues of Reconciliation
of Work and Family Life in Europe.

127

research/studies, in organising events, conferences, in publishing regular reports, in publications and mostly the development of a networking system and cooperation with individuals, agencies, foundations and so on, at national and international level. Among these institutions there should be a prominent position held by entities representing the specific "sensitive" social groups, the interests of which are in the centre of attention of an Observatory. Particular attention should be definitely paid so that there are equal opportunities of information for everyone, especially for special or vulnerable groups (e.g. disabled people, special groups of women threatened by social exclusion, the imprisoned, etc.), and thus avoid the involuntary, but often, reproduction of forms of social exclusion regarding certain groups of the population in the field of information.

Observatory for the reconciliation/harmonisation of family and professional life of the working people, especially women

The aim of the Observatory of the Reconciliation/Harmonisation of Family and Professional Life of the Working People, especially Women, in essence and above all a centre of documentation, is the collection, processing and utilisation of qualitative and quantitative data that are connected to this important social demand in the Republic of Cyprus, with the simultaneous dissemination of relevant information, good practices and positive examples as well as the creation (design – realisation) and submission of similar researches, studies and suggestions to the State and whoever they may concern, with a simultaneous development of networks of corporate relations with socio-economic institutions and public services at both national and international level. At the same time, the Observatory aims at dealing successfully with the lack of centrally planned policy for the Reconciliation/Harmonisation of Family and Professional Life, as well as the systematic and organised assessment of the implementation of reconciliation policies, so that the dissemination of the results of the Observatory actions contribute decisively to improving women's position and on the other hand to formulating and developing positive policies towards families and couples (www.kethi.gr). This specific institution is particularly addressed to employing organisations, economic and social partners, structures that promote issues of gender equality and equal opportunities, women's organisations, researchers of similar issues, any person that might be interested or the entire society.

It is noted that the need for the creation and operation of such an observatory was evident in Cyprus after the realisation of measure 2.1 of CI EQUAL regarding the Reconciliation. Within its frame interesting researches, studies, guides, scientific tools and sensitisation exercises were developed, important material in other words, but also numerous good practices that could be optimised in the future and that reinforce the Observatory already since its first steps. More specifically the objectives of the Observatory are:

- To create a mechanism of consultation and cooperation between institutions, organisations and individuals involved in any way in the process of tackling the phenomenon.
- To examine/map the problem and to assess its quantitative and qualitative dimensions.
- To contribute to a most effective planning of the organisation and operation of services/structures of relevant Counselling through the dissemination of information.
- To offer reliable, in time documentation of quantitative and qualitative data related to the achievement of the Reconciliation.
- To collect, assess and utilize quantitative and qualitative data regarding the Reconciliation.
- To compare data and objectively assess Cyprus' progress towards the achievement of the Reconciliation.
- To transfer and disseminate good practices and models as well as to exchange experiences, know-how and information between Cypriot institutions and European or other international institutions.

Thoughts and Notes on the Issues of Reconciliation
of Work and Family Life in Europe.

129

- To improve the cognitive basis on which the national strategy and the actions for the reconciliation are formed.
- To analyse and interpret data resulting in the framework of the Observatory, either by primary research and studies or provided by affiliated institutions.
- To formulate specific suggestions to the State, various social actors, institutions of equality, businesses, etc.
- To monitor and support the development of the field of Information and Communication Technologies.
- To compose work groups and to form views with institutions, social partners, special scientists, independent authorities and other natural or legal persons that are interested.
- To search for and record good practices from Greece and the rest of Europe.
- To disseminate the knowledge of the above to society.
- To represent Cyprus in European and International Fora.
- To contribute, through suggestions, in the work of the statutory public institution for the Strategy of Gender Equality and Equal Opportunities of the Cypriot Republic.
- To contribute in the elimination of stereotypes, attitudes and behaviours regarding gender equality.

Apart from the above, the objectives include the design and construction of an organised Data Base that will host the available knowledge and will contribute to their processing and answering various questions, as well as the construction of a bilingual web page (Greek and English) that will contribute to communication, action coordination and publicity. The Scientific Committee of the Observatory takes on the responsibility of the construction, monitoring and coordination. Both are central means towards the realisation of the objectives of the Observatory (www.kethi.gr).It is obvious that the ideological/philosophical background of the specific framework is based for starters on gender perspective and the protection of women's human rights. It distinguishes between the terms of "sex" and "gender" and socially defines the different roles, attitudes and behaviours between men and women. *"It recognises the different status and position between man and women that are socially and not biologically determined. It supports that women's limited access to matters of property and control, political participation, work, etc., is caused to the roles ascribed to them and consequently marginalize them from material and non-material resources. It regards the interaction between sex, class and nationality as particularly important. Furthermore, it develops policies of prevention and management of the problem based on gender experiences of men and women, but it also recognises the diverse impact of policies on men and women"* (www.kethi.gr).

Categories of services of the Observatory:
The services of the Observatory are distinguished in the following categories:

the provision of information regarding the achievement of the Reconciliation in Cyprus, through the collection of relevant quantitative and qualitative data and their processing.

the planning and realisation of primary research, which according to their range is carried out by either third parties through competition or internally by the Observatory staff. (At the same time it collects studies conducted by affiliated institutions and performs quantitative and qualitative secondary analyses.)

the provision of counselling services and the formulation of specific proposals and suggestions to concerned parties of the public and private sector regarding issues that relate to the Reconciliation.

(1) the formation of an international network of information and exchange of experiences regarding issues of the Reconciliation.

the assumption of the role of the agency responsible for the coordination and formulation of suggestions on critical issues regarding the

Thoughts and Notes on the Issues of Reconciliation
of Work and Family Life in Europe.

131

Reconciliation, by organising work groups and/or discussions between institutions concerned, social partners, special scientists, etc.

The aforementioned actions, which are about to form a field of gathering information and recording the situation, will have a decisive contribution to the operation of a permanent forum between the affiliated and concerned institutions and individuals. This "forum", that will be supplied with the collection and processing of available information from any research and study conducted, as well as from the data processed by the Observatory, will be coordinated by the Scientific Committee. In this way an institutional framework of dialogue development and consultation is actually formed that will involve and activate dialogue between the parties concerned. The database and the *web page* will particularly contribute to this direction. It should be noted however that the collection, organisation and synthesis of all the available knowledge regarding the promotion of the Reconciliation in Cyprus and internationally will include, among others, international contracts, national laws, scientific articles, various national and international policies, the available products of research and statistical data, information and data from institutions of equality, Departments of Women's Studies from various universities, governmental institutions, NGOs and the Media. The results that will arise from the suggested actions are expected to be the following: development of updated information/data on the issue of the Reconciliation, production of documented and assessed knowledge that will contribute to a more effective organisation of educational courses and the conduct of campaigns of information and sensitisation, formation of a unique mechanism of recording the phenomenology of the issue, intervention, instigation and support of actions to the benefit of working people, especially women, cooperation and activation of institutions and individuals that take action in this subject on a national basis and have the experience, activation of wider forces whose overall objective will be the promotion of the Reconciliation, facilitation of access to information, both of governmental and non-governmental (infra)structures.

Because of the material gathered with reliable and effective methodology and its relation to the targets of the operation and according to the aforementioned results that are expected to arise from the operation of the Observatory, at a first level the benefited will have to do with networks connecting relevant European and national institutions, governmental bodies and institutions, International Organisations and NGOs, etc. Apart from that, it will contribute to the work of policy-makers, experts, the officials and advisors of various Ministries, members of NGOs and women's organisations, aiming at locating the strategies of achieving the Reconciliation. At a second level, it will assist the work of members of universities and research institutes by providing theoretic and empirical data. By taking the aspects of this issue related to social and human rights as well as sex discrimination into special consideration, the Observatory and especially the creation of a forum will attempt to reinforce and network various similar initiatives that have been adopted or will be at community and national level in the frame of various areas of policy. It will formulate and reinforce networks connecting relevant European institutions, governmental bodies and institutions, International Organisations and NGOs, those involved in the promotion of the Reconciliation and the development of structures and services of care for families of working parents. Finally, in the frame of full cooperation it will try to receive and give data to and from the European Commission, the European Parliament, especially the Committee of Women's Rights and Equal Opportunities, as well as other Committees dealing with various aspects of these issues at European level. Also, from the Council of Europe, the Committee of the Regions, Eurostat, Europol, Eurojust, etc. With such activity, it is obvious that the Observatory can put the issue of the Reconciliation in Cyprus on a new footing.

Structure of the Observatory

The operation of the Observatory is based on the principles of modern management, resulting in forming the necessary strategy regarding its long-term objectives, the policy that will ensure the success of its pursuits

Thoughts and Notes on the Issues of Reconciliation
of Work and Family Life in Europe.

133

and the necessary relevant planning. The correct division of labour and the departmentation based on specialisation are regarded as critical factors of success and efficiency of the actions of the Observatory. The distribution of responsibilities and their allocation to collective bodies of the institution contributes, among others, to the compilation of the necessary organogram in order to ensure that the actions developed in the frame of the institution tend towards the success of its objectives. Of course, a basic condition for success is the achievement of efficient communication, in vertical and horizontal arrangement of positions, inside the Observatory, but also the communication with concerned agencies outside the institution (Holevas, 1995). More specifically:

1. Human resources

The distinct, profoundly social dimension of an Observatory already since its establishment requires extreme caution during the process of covering its needs in staff both on a short- and long-term basis. At the same time a careful job description is required, with a clear definition of its duties and the place where they will be performed, the time it will completed, the wage given, etc. Regarding both administrative and scientific or other positions, after planning the staff needs of the structure there should be provision regarding not only their acquisition but also their ongoing education and training on matters of Gender Equality and Equal Opportunities and not only those, as it is evident that an Observatory needs high-level staff. The number and terms of employment will depend on the budget of the institution and the will of the co-responsible Ministries, but also the relevant institutional framework. More specifically:

A. The head of the Observatory will be a representative Management Board of nine members, comprising (totally indicatively) of representatives of the following institutions:

- Ministry of Justice and Public Order
- Ministry of Labour and Social Security
- Commissioner for Administration (Ombudsman)

- Institutions of Equality
- Women's Departments of Parties
- Employing agencies
- Trade unions etc.

B. The scientific responsibility and action monitoring as well as the assessment of the course of operation of the Observatory is assumed by the *Scientific Committee*, that is comprised of experts and scientists, specialists in matters of Gender Equality and Equal Opportunities, with a higher participation of women. It is responsible not only for developing, supporting and monitoring actions that will contribute to the documented collection of data and the scientific analysis of the data, but also for all the activities that express the objectives of the institution and point out its scientific adequacy for their fulfilment. It is also responsible for their maintenance, the formulation of rules of operation and the publication of information leaflets and the dissemination of the operation of the Observatory.

C. A Legal Advisor assumes the legal coverage of the decisions and actions of the institution and its bodies.

D. The administrative-financial responsibility and generally the safeguarding of the smooth operation of the Observatory is assumed by a *Manager* with proven experience and sensitivity on gender issues.

E. The staff of the Observatory is comprised of individuals of high qualifications and increased sensitivity on gender matters – researchers, information specialists and administrative-financial staff which is necessary within its frame. In any case the Management Board in cooperation with the Scientific Committee will proceed to the description of the current work positions and the required professional skills for any position as mentioned above.

2. Departments:

The Observatory, like all similar organisations, should be divided in Departments, each one specializing in performing certain tasks

Thoughts and Notes on the Issues of Reconciliation
of Work and Family Life in Europe.

135

(Departmentation). This specialisation involves all the individuals that belong to a department and is characterised by the task performed. It contributes to the obtainment of knowledge and skills, to the familiarisation with the work place and all the technological and other means that are used (Holevas, 1995). The departmentation, as known, is performed based on certain criteria. In this case it is preferable to be done based on the distinction of the operation of each department (operational distinction), which is the most common 17. Each department (operation) may be further divided in depth according to the needs of the institution in .subdivisions. More specifically the following division is suggested:

A. Department of Studies and Research
B. Department of Supporting Services
C. Department of Administrative Services
D. Department of Financial Services
E. Department of Information

It is noted that within the frame of the Observatory and especially the Department of Supporting Services there are:

The "Online Statistics" service of the Observatory, which offers the possibility of dynamic presentation and production of statistical data. Through this service any person concerned is offered free access to the statistical data of research conducted by the Observatory regarding the Reconciliation.

The Archive of Studies and Reports. The Observatory, as the central information agency about the Reconciliation/Harmonisation of Family and Professional Life of Working People and especially Women, develops an archive of research/studies conducted by Greek and foreign institutions regarding the course of the country not only to the achievement of the Reconciliation. The same Archive includes the Reports issued by the Observatory and similar institutions of the Republic of Cyprus, the European Union, etc.

<u>The Good Practices Archive</u> in the priority fields of the Reconciliation, aiming at highlighting the progress made both at a European and international level, since the transfer and dissemination of best methods and practices and the support of experience exchange between Cypriot institutions. An interesting similar experience of operation of the above subdivisions is offered by the administrative structure of the Observatory of Information Society in Greece (<u>http://www.observatory.gr/page/default.asp?id=4</u>).

3. Organogram

The organogram demonstrates the anatomy of the institution, its vertical and horizontal structure. It shows the levels of administration, the executive bodies, the assisting departments and its main collective bodies. Its objective is informative, critical and ethical. The following organogram demonstrates the organisational and internal structure of the Observatory.

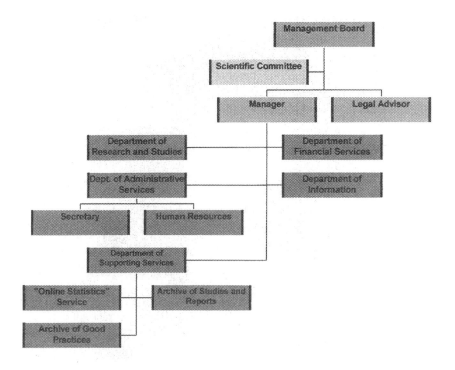

Thoughts and Notes on the Issues of Reconciliation
of Work and Family Life in Europe.

137

3.9. *Afterward*

Based on the above, the emphasis placed by the European Union on the adoption of measures and practices that enhance the combination of private and professional life becomes understandable [18]. Of great importance is also the provision of maternity leaves (paid, if possible), as well as other parental leaves and also with the adoption of incentives for men, so that they are motivated to receive them (Warin, Solomon, Lewis & Langford, 1999). In this way women will not be forced to stop working for good, during or after the postpartum period and it will be possible for men to assume their share of responsibilities, thus preventing the loss of valuable female labour force. Towards this there is a decisive contribution from the creation of an advanced system of care structures for the children and the elderly, so that women (who are usually burdened with their care) may continue to work without distractions if they wish so. Another parameter concerns securing the provision of quality care for children, elderly and other dependant members of the family, so that women who bear the burden of their care can seek work, keep quality jobs and advance to responsible positions, utilizing their creativity and skills outside the family too. This second parameter is directly linked to the democratic-social demands for the redistribution of the social roles of the genders within the family (with the adoption of social maternity) and also with the redistribution of the inter-family time in favour of the women. If this does not happen, many of the positive measures proposed (e.g. part-time employment, flexible working hours, tele-work etc) might very well work against women in the long run, reproducing anachronistic stereotypes in modern conditions.

However, the efforts that are made at a European and national level (European Union, member state governments, businesses, trade unions, employees) for the reconciliation of family and professional life, the development of human resources and the achievement of business profit, are likely to fail if they are not combined with the development of social awareness through social policy and change in mentality. At the same time, the defence and expansion of full-time employment has to be the aim of the reforms for the reconciliation of family and professional life, although it is often omitted from the relevant studies, as it offers stability, permanence, equal participation of the sexes, therefore occupational entrenchment and assertable rights. The implementation of "flexible" forms of employment, which have caused much discussion and are often advertised as the only solution to unemployment, cannot be done without cost for the worker. Research reveals that often employees accept to increase their working hours in order to secure employment. In Finland, for instance, employees tend to work more than average hours especially when their children are young (even though they have the ability to work with more favourable hours). In Italy, a form of employment that is being promoted is the "on-call job", in which workers are hired on an open contract and few work rights and are called to work in hard conditions completely dependent on their employers. Consequently, in any similar proposal a lot of attention is required, as in the frame of implementation the safeguarding of employees rights should be taken into consideration.

On the other hand, the reconciliation of family and professional life should be related to combating unemployment, to the elimination of occupational segregation and obstacles in evolution and to the incorporation of the gender aspect in all policies, practices and measures for supporting employment. In order to achieve this goal, what is needed is constant effort and encouragement towards the State, but also to the socio-economic organisations that are involved in this matter one way or the other. Of vital importance, according to the present study, are the possibilities provided by the collective negotiations and by extension of the collective labour agreements in promoting equal opportunities and the reconciliation of family and professional life. Especially in cases where there is a legislative gap or the law provisions are inadequate, the collective agreements are called to protect employees and to promote

Thoughts and Notes on the Issues of Reconciliation
of Work and Family Life in Europe.

139

their interests at the work place. This estimation, however, does not hold back the unpleasant finding that the negotiations themselves are likely to perpetuate unequal distribution of power between the sexes by the absence of women in them – unfortunately a phenomenon across Europe – with a further consequence, the absence of gender aspect from the collective agreements [19].

In the European Parliament important proposals are submitted regarding the improvement of balancing family and professional life. Europe should tackle a three-fold challenge: shrinking active population, low birth rates and increasing elderly population. At the same time, the increasing world economic competition demands a more flexible and mobile labour force. According to the above, consequences are more perceptible on women, who are obliged to choose between career and children, because there is a lack of flexible work arrangements and care services or because gender stereotypes are persistent and the distribution of family obligations with men is unequal. The progress that has been made with women's participation in basic sectors of the economy and society, such as research and education, is not fully reflected in women's position in the labour market. It is a loss of human resources that the European Union in general and Cyprus in particular do not have the luxury to miss.

In Cyprus the possibility of combining the conflicting demands between paid employment (not to mention a career) and the changing personal needs and non-professional duties often requires a huge effort in part of the individual, the woman in particular. This incessant struggle for the control of time has been mostly left to the exclusive responsibility of working people, especially women, even though it is gradually flagged as a priority sector for policy implementation in macro and micro level. The combination of family and professional life is a fundamental component of gender perspective in the European strategy regarding employment and the process for social inclusion (Mouriki, 2005). It aims at promoting a more cohesive society by ensuring favourable conditions for men and women's entrance, re-entrance and stay in the labour market. At the same time it is related to the development of human resources, the achievement of business profit, but also transnational socio-economic growth. This important demand of our times urges the acceptance of the fact that whatever regulations towards the Reconciliation must acknowledge

1. that participation in family care is an equal responsibility of both men and women and to serve them to the same extent.
2. that a balanced participation of men and women both in the labour market and family life is a necessary element to the development of the society and that motherhood, fatherhood and children's rights are essential social values protected by the society, the member states and the European Union.
3. that facilitating women in successfully combining their professional and family obligations is both their right and a precondition of their evolution.

In the framework of Transnational Partnership SEMELI the D.P. "Reconciliation Intervention" and ELANI (Cyprus) developed interesting and innovative activities in the sector of planning and implementing actions that promote the equality of social genders with emphasis on the reconciliation/harmonization of the professional and family life in the area of the local administration organizations and the businesses. The purpose of these actions was to set equality policies as a priority and to launch a debate in the context of the local administrations and businesses, and further, on all levels, to explore and implement methods and measures that could better promote the equal participation of men and women in work and the family, so that they obtain the maximum from these top expressions of life and improve their living conditions. The benefits from such an effort will be important both on a personal and social level.

Thoughts and Notes on the Issues of Reconciliation
of Work and Family Life in Europe.

141

The current survey reaffirmed the observations of its theoretical framework and ratifies respective conclusions of surveys conducted in other European and other countries. The conclusions also indicate the horizontal and vertical gender division of the Cypriot labor market, and the strong, resistant and even patriarchal structures of the Cypriot family, despite the apparent tendency towards change. It is obvious that it is women who bear the main burden of inter-family responsibilities in Cyprus, linked to what we are used to calling "household", and also the care and upbringing of children and the care of other dependant members. And if it is not the working mother, it is always a grandmother or house maid that is other women, in the predominant ideological framework which links the female being with the household and the duties and responsibilities emanating from it. So, it is not by chance that the women of the sample have less personal time compared to the men of the sample and their partners and show an increased interest in the implementation of equality strategies. Nevertheless, in the framework of the specific survey a new type of father/spouse begins to emerge, which modern bibliography calls the "new involved father", who is characterized by a change in attitude and understands his paternal capacity as "a more responsible and equivalent relationship with the woman, during which the duties and satisfaction 'within' and 'outside' the house are shared equally". The attitude of being a family, rather than having a family is more apparent." (K.E.Θ.I. 2007). The fact produces optimism, but not complacency. The leading father and husband model continues to be that of a good provider and not rarely the "bad" and/or "uninterested" one, which leads to maintaining and reproducing gender inequalities within the family. From the aforementioned, it becomes obvious that the demand for the redistribution of social roles in the family context, directly linked to the redistribution of inter-family time in favor of women as well and the achievement of social maternity by both parents, is in fact a deeply democratic - and thus political - demand of our times, concerns both genders and is the basis and precondition for the success of any relevant measures the state undertakes to implement or any family- and women-friendly strategies the businesses are called upon to apply. Regarding the latter, it is nevertheless stressed that any anachronistic family structure cannot be allowed to be an alibi for slacking and delays by the state to respond to the EU call, forming the necessary institutional framework, securing the necessary funds and organizing the necessary campaigns and other information/awareness of the public opinion activities. The businesses on the other hand must assume their social responsibility by moving toward the choice and implementation of inter-business reconciliation strategies, linking them with the development of human resources and business profit.

In recent years there has been an evident participation of businesses in family policies and the relevant sensitisation of a number of employers appears to be raised. It has to do with measures of a limited range that do not involve the great majority of people employed in the private sector (Gasouka, 2007). Even the current system of social security and welfare can neither be regarded as adequate or efficient, as it is limited to economic benefits and tax reductions. At the same time the conflict between workers' family and professional life is stronger, especially when it regards highly qualified parents who are totally committed to their professional life or in general the so-called dual-career families. In order to tackle with this problem, all EU countries have developed policies for the reconciliation of family and work either at a legislative level or by the initiative of large businesses, the help of trade unions, feminist or other organisations that aim at sensitising the public opinion in matters like the irrational expansion of the work hours, the role of the father, etc. More specifically, where businesses are concerned, employers have started to realise that the balance between family and professional life contributes to a decrease in sex differences and quality improvement in the work place. However the most important aspect is that policies of harmonisation between family and career forms "win-win" situations: a) workers enjoy a better work environment and gain more satisfaction and self confidence, b) businesses benefit from motivated, ambitious staff that has less absences and more productivity, c) the harmonisation helps

Thoughts and Notes on the Issues of Reconciliation
of Work and Family Life in Europe.

143

create a flexible economy that uses all its human resources constructively. Therefore, the measures for harmonising the family/professional life of workers, that should be combined with other measures of social policy, should aim at developing social awareness and the economy. As it is obvious, the above remarks regard the public sphere of life and the role that state and other socio-economic bodies and organizations are called upon to play jointly, at a national and European level. However, the success of the effort, the achievement of the much desired harmonization of work and family life presupposes substantial changes in the individual / collective perceptions – stances – beliefs for the social roles of genders in society and family. It is absolutely certain that without re-distributing the roles within the family amongst adult members and the under aged members, the achievement of social maternity with the active and balanced participation of men as well in the upbringing and care of children, but also to secure time within the family in favor of women as well, as we can see also from the on-the spot-surveys below, women will continue to enter the labor market under unequal terms, they will experience daily disputes between their own needs, expectations, desires and everything that their society has traditionally / patriarchically assigned in the form of exclusively female / mother duties, having as a result often either their removal from work or the effort to claim a job, either their resignation from their professional aspirations and efforts to be promoted. It is however known that until today, the majority of women that live under the regime of this conflict often experience a constant agony relating to their identity, the role or roles that are called upon to fulfill and they are afraid that they do not know how, that is, at the same time they experience regrets and guilt and they form the most obvious "false conscience" which has as a result for their social, material and natural life to be transformed into duties – recipes that originate from a patriarchically "fabricated knowledge" which every woman must implement. Moreover, every failure constitutes a personal failure, it is a failure of a woman that did not prove to be skilful, that did not meet up to the social requirements with serious repercussions for her self-esteem but also regarding her acceptance from her family – and not only – environment. As such, if this unequal until now, situation of women inside the family as well does not change, if as it is correctly said, democracy does not flourish inside the family, everything women have conquered in the public sphere shall remain mortgaged.

At the same time it should be understood that family democracy is undermined by the exhaustion and frustration caused to women by occupational segregation inside the family, the abandonment of professional ambitions or the public sphere itself that often is imposed by this division. Never before in history has the demand of redefining the social roles inside the family been so imperatively critical. Equally important appears to be the redefinition of the paternal role as well as its emergence as a fundamental coordinate of family democracy and equality. At the same time, what also results from the above is the defining role of the State, that knows very well that there cannot be economic growth, social cohesion, even democracy, if women remain at the margins of labour, an eternally reserve labour army, and if workers of both sexes experience a conflicting, stressful relation between their family and professional life (Pillinger, 2002). Thus it is not strange that issues of gender equality and equal opportunities, with emphasis on the reconciliation/harmonisation of family and professional life, are already high on the agenda of the national governments and the European Union. The creation and successful, efficient operation of an Observatory of Reconciliation is bound to have an important contribution to the relevant efforts of Cypriot State and its institutions.

Thoughts and Notes on the Issues of Reconciliation
of Work and Family Life in Europe.

145

NOTES

1. The statistical source of the report of EGGSIE for the Commission is: European Childcare Strategies, Statistical Annex

2. Social Welfare Service, *from Public Allowance*, Programme Aim 3, ESF (A pancyprian study has already begun).

3. Apart from *Elani*, two other development collaborations, *Pandora* and *New Routes for Women,* are preparing studies.

4. Organizations from Cyprus do not participate in the following interstate programmes. The comparative results, however, provide directly to the expansion of the relevant research in Cyprus:

a) *Care Work in Europe*, 2001, EC Fifth Framework Programme (cross-national study)

b) *Family life and professional work: Conflict and synergy*, EC 5th Framework Research Programme

c) *Transitions, Gender, parenthood and the changing European workplace: Young adults negotiating the work-family boundary*, EC 5th Framework Research Programme

d) *Households, Work and Flexibility*, Fifth Framework Research Programme, HWF Research Consortium.

5. "Woman and higher managerial positions in the banking and semi-governmental sector"

6. Interview with Mrs. Alexia Papadopoulou, Legal Advisor and Member of the INC Board, Limassol, Thursday 14/2/2006

7. The timetable for public and community nursery schools is 7.45am - 1.05pm for children aged 3-6. That of private schools varies, with many operating until 1pm and others with additional afternoon times, which rarely cover the working time of employees in various sectors of the economy. Many unemployed women admit to officers of the Ministry of Labor that it is too costly and impossible to work, due to the cost and timetable of nursery schools (Debate with Labor Department officers).

8. The economic activities not included due to non-representation of the two genders are: agriculture, fishing, mining and construction. Furthermore, the categories "other services", private households and exterritorial organizations were excluded (Workforce Study 2004).

9. Legislative equalityy does not in any case anticipate of safeguard the equal access and evolution of the two sexes in the labour market. Besides, reforms of this kind and wider social changes are very hard to realise in such a short period of time (Athanasiadou, Petropoulou & Mimikou, 2001).

10. Working time and its organisation are one of the most important problems that must be dealt with, for the combination of family and professional life. At a Community level there is Council Directive 97/81/EC of 15 December 1997, *concerning the Framework Agreement on part-time work concluded by UNICE, CEEP and the ETUC and Council Directive 93/104/EC of 23 November 1993, concerning certain aspects of the organisation of working time,* amended by Directive 2000/34/EC of the European Parliament and of the Council of 22 June 2000, concerning certain aspects of the organisation of working time to cover sectors and activities excluded from that Directive. The first of these Directives invites member states to adopt the necessary measures so that, in compliance with the general principles relating to the protection of the safety and health of workers, the weekly working hours are limited and the average working time for each seven-day period, including overtime, does not exceed 48 hours (www.kethi.gr).

11. In order to achieve the combination of family and professional life there have to be certain legal rules, as well as public structures of care that the State and regional and local governments must offer to the citizens for the coverage of the needs of dependent individuals. At a community level there is a special legal document, the Recommendation of the Council of 31 March 1992 *regarding childcare.* In this way initiatives are taken aiming at encouraging the flexibility and diversity of childcare services. Moreover, it encourages the possibility of access to child care services enabling parents who are working, following a course of education or training in order to obtain employment or are seeking employment or a course of education or training in order to obtain employment to have as much access as possible to local child-care services. The services are offered at prices affordable to parents; the needs of parents

Thoughts and Notes on the Issues of Reconciliation
of Work and Family Life in Europe.

147

and children are taken into account when access to services is determined; the services are available in all areas and regions of Member States, both in urban areas and in rural areas; the services are accessible to children with special needs, and to children in single-parent families, and meet the needs of such children.

12. The problem of coincidence of the working hours of the public and private services is mainly a result of women's increased participation in the labour market. In general, the working hours of the services (such as banks, shops, administrative authorities, the health system and schools) coincide with the working hours, resulting in hindering the combination of family and professional life. Public services have even less flexible hours, while the opening hours of the shops have become more flexible under consumer pressure. The same applies for school hours. Schools usually are open less hours than businesses and this creates a gap between the parents' work obligations and the care of their children. Only in the Scandinavian countries, where there are many childcare structures, organized and funded by the local authorities, this gap is bridged by full day care services and centres for creative occupation of children.

13. The countries of the European Union have a number of projects and plans to achieve this reconciliation. In general, the measures adopted by either the state or the businesses, or non-governmental organisations pertain mostly to women and their difficulty in combining their family obligations with work. Broadly speaking, the adopted policies mostly include the arrangement and flexibility of work time and childcare. Great emphasis is placed by businesses and organisations on facilitating women to successfully combine their family and professional obligations. Several actions are funded to this direction, such as the reinforcement of the operational cost of structures within the business for keeping and/or creatively occupying the workers' children, telework and the adaptation of administration models to the models of corporate social responsibility. The expected results from the pilot application are regarded to cause the required changes in the inside of businesses, so that working women are not obstructed in their professional choices and to better manage their working time – on the other hand, businessmen are also expected to value the benefit from the increase in productivity, the limitation of phenomena of absence or employment termination as well as inability to assume new responsibilities.

14. The Observatory studies the extent and progression of phenomena and demonstrations of racism, xenophobia and anti-Semitism, it analyses their causes, consequences and results and examines examples of good practice. To this end, it collects, records and analyses data gathered by research centres of the member states, the community institutional bodies, non-governmental organisations or international organisations. Apart from these, it has to form and coordinate a "European network of information on racism and xenophobia" (RAXEN).

15. Observatory of Equal Opportunities of Spain. Formed in 2000 and belonging to the Ministry of Labour, it is an organisation whose fundamental objectives are the collection, analysis and dissemination of periodical information on the condition of women in the country and the assessment of the society regarding gender equality. Based on the resulting data, it aims at planning policies, actions and activities that will point out the importance of this information in different spheres of life. A significant part of its actions, which are diffused in all of Spain, regard issues of reconciliation of women's family and professional life and the adjustment of legislation to this aim. Several Autonomous Communities including Melilla, six women's organisations, INJUVE and representatives from every Ministry participate in the Observatory. In Spain there are corresponding equivalent institutions in the Autonomous Communities as well.

16. Observatory for Women's Health. Formed in 2006, this initiative started from the suggestions gathered in the Madrid Statement of the European Panel on Gender Mainstreaming Health in 2001, with the support of the WHO Regional Office for Europe. The Statement examines the acknowledgement on behalf of the health authorities the biological differences and the social roles between men and women, and the recognition of gender as a determinant and the need for changes in the organisational culture of health services. The objectives of the Observatory are the collection and dissemination of information aiming at improving the knowledge regarding the causes and dimensions of differences between men and women located in the field of health (e.g. the use of the right indicators). The Observatory also processes

Thoughts and Notes on the Issues of Reconciliation
of Work and Family Life in Europe.

149

and disseminates studies, analyses towards the introduction of innovations in the frame of health organisations related to primary health care, training and research. The Observatory offers help and technical support to the Interterritorial Council of SNS (Sistema Nacional de Salud) in developing indicators, methodology and procedures that will allow the analysis of the reformatory policies of health of the SNS, from a gender perspective, in collaboration with Women's Institute.

17. Other forms of Departmentation are the division according to services, the geographical division, the division based on the user category of the products, etc.

18. Another reason for reconciling family and professional life is that nowadays most young people work long hours resulting in delaying the creation of a new family. Furthermore, there is a large percentage of young people who, due to unemployment or low wages, do not have the necessary resources to start a family and have children. This in turn results in low birth rates.

19. The new institutional framework for the collective labour agreements provides more freedom for bargaining than in the past and offers the ability to escape the passive solution of the provision of leaves towards more active practices. The history of the collective labour agreements has demonstrated that there is a dynamic of improving decisions towards equal opportunities and the reconciliation of family and professional life. The encouragement and reinforcement of female presence in collective bargaining will have a significant contribution towards equality and social justice.

BIBLIOGRAPHY

Abrahamson, Peter and Cecilie Wehner. 2006. "Family and/or Work in Europe?" *Journal of Comparative Family Studies* 37(2):153-17

Adema, William. 2005. "Volume 1 Australia, Denmark, and the Netherlands."in *Babies and Bosses, Reconciling Work and Family Life*"Volume 1 Australia, Denmark, and theNetherlands." Pairs: OECD Publishing.1.

Andersen T 1997, Do institutions matter? Convergence and national diversity in the restructuring of employment in British and Danish banking, European Journal of Industrial Relations, Vol. 3, n° 1, p. 107-124.

Andersen T 2000 Banking and insurance sectors - Euro-FIET, Transfer, European Review of Labour and Research, Vol. 6, n° 1, p. 110-114.

Anker R. (1997), *Theories of Occupational Segregation by Sex: an Overview, International Labour Review,* Vol. 136, No. 3, Geneva.

Argyrou P (2006), *Reconciliation of Work and Family Obligations and Labor Market*,Website:http://www.alkistisequal.gr/inst/alkistis/gallery/Training/Lecture%20of%20trainer.doc / www.alkistis-equal.gr

Bond, S., Hyman, J. & S. Wise, 2002, *Family friendly working? Putting policy into practice,* The Policy Press, Bristol

Bielenski, H., Bosch, G. & Wagner, A.,(2002), W*orking time preferences in sixteen European countries,* European Foundation for the Improvement of Living and Working Conditions, Luxembourg: Office for Official Publications of the European Communities

Bond, S., Hyman, J. & S. Wise, (2002), *Family friendly working? Putting policy into practice,* The Policy Press, Bristol

Borchorst, Anette. 2001. "Still Friendly: Danish Women and Welfare State Restructuring." *Social Politics* 8(2):203-205.

Bosch, G.; Haipeter, Th.; Voss-Dahm, D. ; Wagner, A. 2001, Changes in employment practice in the service sector. Findings from five sectors and ten countries, ETUI Report, No 71, Brussels

Boulin, J. Y., (1997), "From working time to city time: the case for a single approach to time policies", *Transfer,* vol.4

Brodmann, Stefanie, Gosta Esping-Anderson and Maia Guell. 2007. "When Fertility is Bargained: Second Births in Denmark and Spain." *European Sociological Review* 223(5):599-613

Campos Lima M. and Naummann, R. 2000: Social Pacts in Portugal: From Comprehensive Policy Programmes to the Negotiation of Concrete Industrial Relations Reforms? in Fajertag and Pochet (2000), ibid.

Crompton, R.; Birkelund GE 2000, Employment and caring in British and Norwegian banking: an exploration through individual careers, Work, Employment and Society, Vol. 14, n° 2, p. 331-352.

Thoughts and Notes on the Issues of Reconciliation
of Work and Family Life in Europe.

153

Central Intelligence Agency. 2008. "World Factbook-Denmark Country Profile.", Retrieved 03/01 (www.cia.gov/library/publication/ [the-world-factbook/geos/da.html](http://www.cia.gov/library/publication/the-world-factbook/geos/da.html)).

Collins, J., (2001). *Lever 5 Leadership. The Triumph of Humility and Fierce Resolve. Harvard Business Review,* Jan., pp. 19-28

Communication from the Commission of 21 February 1996, 'Incorporating equal opportunities for women and men into all Community policies and activities' COM(96) 67 final.

Communication from the Commission to the Council and the European Parliament - Framework Strategy on Gender Equality - Work Programme for 2001 (COM (2001)119 final) and Commission Staff Working Paper: Work programme for 2001 of each Commission service for the implementation of the Framework Strategy on Gender Equality (SEC(2001) 382), see: http://europa.eu.int/comm/employment_social/ [equ_opp/gms_en.html](http://europa.eu.int/comm/employment_social/equ_opp/gms_en.html)

Commission of the European Communities, Communication from the Commission to the Council, the European Parliament, the European Economic and Social Committee and the Committee of the Regions, Mid-Term Review of the Social Policy Agenda, Brussels, 2.6.2003, COM(2003)312 final.

Commission of the European Communities, Report from the Commission to the Council, the European Parliament, the European Economic and Social Committee and the Committee of the Regions, *on equality between men and women,* Brussels, 14.2.2005, COM(2005) 44 final.

Communication from the Commission to the Council, the European Parliament, the Economic and Social Committee and the Committee of the Regions, *Towards a Community Framework Strategy on Gender Equality (201-2005), COM (2000) 335* final.

Committee of European Communities, Announcement of the Commission to the Council, the European Parliament, the Economic and Social Committee and the Committee of the Regions, "Towards a Community Framework Strategy on Gender Equality (2001-2005)", Brussels, 7-6-2000.

Council Decision of 22 July 2003 *on guidelines for the employment policies of the Member States* (2003/578/EC).

Council of Employment and Social Policy Ministers (2000), *Resolution regarding the balanced participation of women and men in the professional and family life.*

Dex, S., Smith, C. and Winter, S (2001). *Effects of family friendly policies on business performance,* Research Paper, The Judge Institute of Management Studies: University of Cambridge.

Den D. & Den L, (2001), *Work-family arrangements in organisations. A cross-national study in the Netherlands, Italy, United Kingdom and Sweden,* London: Rozenberg Publishers.

Department of Trade & Industry, *Work Life Balance. The business case,* Scotland Office, 2001

Dulk, Laura D. and Anneke van Doorne-Huiskes. 2007. "Social Policy in Europe: its Impact on Families and Work." Pp. 35-57 in *Women, Men, Work and Family in Europe*, edited by R.

Thoughts and Notes on the Issues of Reconciliation
of Work and Family Life in Europe.

155

Crompton, Susan Lewis and Clare Lyonette. New York: Macmillan. ESS round 2, R Jowell and the Central Co-ordinating Team, European Social Survey 2004/2005:*Technical Report,* London: Centre for Comparative Social Surveys, City University (2005)

Ellingsaeter, Anne L. and Arnlaug Leire, eds. 2006. *Politicising Parenthood in Scandinavia: Gender relations in welfare states.* Great Britain: The Policy Press.

Ellingsaeter, Anne L. 1998. "Dual Breadwinner Societies: Provider Models in the Scandinavian Welfare States." *Acta Sociologica* 41(1):59-73.

European Commission (1996,1997,1998,1999,2000,2001) *Annual Report on Equal Opportunities for Women and Men in the European Union.* Luxemburg: Office for Official Publications of the European Communities.

European Commission of Employment & Social Affairs, (2002). *Social Agenda,* Issue no.1, April

European Commission, (2006), *A Roadmap for Equality Between Women and Men 2006-2010(2006),* Directorate-General for Employment, Social Affairs and Equal Opportunities, Unit G.1, Manuscript completed in April

European Foundation for the Improvement of Living and Working Conditions, (2000), *Equal opportunities, collective bargaining and the European employment strategy,* Available at http://eurofound.europa.eu/eiro/2000/05/study/tn0005402s.html

European Foundation for the Improvement of Living and Working Conditions, (2006), *Reconciliation of work and family life and collective bargaining in the European Union, An analysis of EIRO articles.* Available at www.eiro.eurofound.eu.int

European Observatory on Family Matters,. (2000). *Family Observer,* no.3, Brussels

Evans, J. M., (2000). *Firms' contribution to the reconciliation between work and family life, Labour Market and Social Policy Occasional Papers,* OECD

European Commission, 2000a, Social Policy Agenda, COM (2000) 379 of 28/06/2000.

European Commission, 2000b: Report on Social Protection in Europe, 1999, Bruxelles.

European Foundation for the Improvement of Living and Working Conditions, 2002, "Quality of work and employment in Europe. Issues and challenges", Foundation paper, no.1, February, Dublin

European Observatory on Family Matters, 2000 "Family Observer", no.3, Brussels.

Factors for Success: a compedium of social partner initiatives relating to the Employment Guidelines of the European Employment Strategy, CEEP, ETUC, & UNICE/UEAPME, November 2000, Mimeo

Evans J. M., (2002). *Work/Family Reconciliation, Gender Wage Equity and Occupational Segregation: The Role of Firms and Public Policy,* Canadian Public Policy – Analyse de Politiques, Vol. XXVIII, Supplement/No. Special 1.

Thoughts and Notes on the Issues of Reconciliation
of Work and Family Life in Europe.

157

Fagan, C. & Hebson, G. (2004), *'Making work pay', debates from a gender perspective: A comparative review of some recent policy reforms in thirty European Countries.* Manchester: European Work and Employment Research Centre.

Fagan, C., 2001, *Gender, employment and working time preferences in Europe,* European Foundation for the Improvement of Living and Working Conditions, Luxembourg: Office for Official Publications of the European Communities

Fine-Davis, Margret, Jeanne Fagnani, Dino Giovannini, Lis Hojgaard and Hilary Clarke. 2004. "Chapter 4 Denmark." Pp. 41 in *Fathers and Mothers: Dilemmas of the Work-Life Balance.* Dordrecht: Kluwer Academic Publishers.

Gasouka M., (2004), Sociological Approaches of Gender, Athens: Delfi

Gasouka M., (2007), *Guide for Equality and Reconciliation of Work and Family Life,* SEMELI, Melilla-Athens-Nicosia

Gasouka M., (2008), *Conciliations Plans for the Harmonization of the Professional and Family Life,* ELANI, Nicosia.

Gonas, L., 2002 "Work-life balance in Sweden", paper presented at the conference organised by the European Industrial Relations Review on *Work-life balance and diversity in European industrial relations,* London, June 21 & 22.

Gornick, Janet C. and Marcia K. Meyers. 2003. *Families that Work: Policies for Reconciling Parenthood and Employment.* New York: Russell Sage Foundation.

Gupta, Nabanita D. and Nina Smith. 2002. "Children and Career Interruptions: The Family Gap in Denmark." *Economica* 69:609-629.

Halvorsen, Rune and Per H. Jensen. 2004. "Activation in Scandinavian Welfare Policy." *European Societies* 6(4):461-483.

Henderson, D., 2000 "Call centres: issues surrounding women workers in Great Britain", report submitted to UNI Finance, September.

Hojgaard, Lis. 1997. "Working fathers--caught in the web of the symbolic order of gender." *Acta Sociologica* 40(3):245-261.

Institute of Management & U.M.I.S.T., 2001, "Quality of Working Life". Report into managerial working life in the U.K., February

International Labor Office. *Decent work in Denmark : employment, social efficiency and economic security.* 2003. Geneva: ILO.

Jorgensen, Per S. 1991. "Out-of-home care in Denmark." *Child Welfare* 70:107-113.

Kokkinou M. (2008), "The Touch of the Teachers with the European Programmes and their Stereotypes about Others", MegaPoster Publications, Athens. (In Greek).

Kokkinou M. (2008), "Pontiac Migrants from Ex-Soviet Union at School and Possible Factors of their Social Exclusion", Doctoral Dissertation, Panteion University, Athens. (In Greek).

Kremer, Monique. 2006. "The Politics of Ideals of Care: Danish and Flemish Child Care Policy Compared." *Social Politics* 13(2):261-285.

Thoughts and Notes on the Issues of Reconciliation
of Work and Family Life in Europe.

159

Leitner, Andrea and Angela Wroblewski. 2006. "Welfare States and Work-Life Balance: Can Good Practices Be Transferred from the Nordic Countries to Conservative Welfare States?" *European Societies* 8(2):295-317.

Liapi M., & Tzavara M. (2005)., *Manual for the implementation of equality plans*, Community Initiative Equal, Equal Andromeda, Actions for combating the division in the workplace, Athens

Lewis S. (1997), "Rethinking Employment: An Organizational Culture Change Framework", in S. Lewis and J. Lewis eds, The Work Family Challenge. Rethinking Employment, London, Sage Publications, pp 1-19.

Lewis J., (2002), "Gender and Welfare State Change", European Societies 4 (4), pp 331-357.

Littlewood P., Glorieux I., Jonsson I., (2004) "The Future of Work in Europe", Ashgate Publishing Ltd.

Lilja, R., 2001, *Working time preferences at different phases of life*, European Foundation for the Improvement of Living and Working Conditions, Luxembourg: Office for Official Publications of the European Communities

Mayer G; Andersen T ; Muller M 2001, Employment restructuring and flexibility in Austrian and Danish banking, European Journal of Industrial Relations, Vol. 7, n° 1, p. 71-87.

Manniche, Erik. 1985. *The family in Denmark*. Helsing, Denmark: IPC Print & Press

Martin, Gary and Vladimir Kats. 2003. "Families and Work in Transition in 12 Countries, 1980-2001." *Monthly Labor Review.* 126 (9): 3-31.

Medium-term Community Action Programme for the Provision of Equal Opportunities to Men and Women (1996 - 2000) Exchange, Development and Transfer of Good Practice Information and Experience, *Good Practice in European Union countries in relation to the Better Combination of Family and Professional Life*, Athens 2001

Mermet, E. & S. Lehndorff (eds.), 2002, "New forms of employment in the service economy", E.T.U.I., Report 69, Brussels.

Ministry of Familiy and Consumer Affairs.", Retrieved 03/01, 2008 (http://www.minff.dk/english/the-ministry/).

Moss, Peter and Fred Devon. 2006. "Leave Policies and Research: A Cross-National Overview." *Families and Social Policy: National and International Perspectives* 39:255-285.

Nielson, Lise D. 1991. "Flexibility, Gender, and Local Labour Markets -Some Examples from Denmark." *International Journal of Urban and Regional Research* 15(1):42. Retrieved February 24, 2008 Available: EBSCOHOST SocINDEX.

Official Journal of the European Communities, Treaty of Nice, *Amending the Treaty on European Union, the Treaties establishing the European Communities and certain related acts,* (2001/C/80/01], text at: http://eur-lex.europa.eu/LexUriServ/LexUriServ.do?uri=OJ:C:2001:08 0:0001:0087:EN:PDF

Thoughts and Notes on the Issues of Reconciliation
of Work and Family Life in Europe.

161

Organisation for Economic Co-operation and Development. 2004. "Public Expenditure on Childcare and Early Education Services." (www. oecd.org/dataoecd/44/20/38954032.xls).

"The Organisation of Gender Equality Work in Denmark.", Retrieved 03/04, 2008 (http://www.lige.dk/).

Pamamichael St., *Research to record social welfare structures,* A.S. "Reconciliation Intervention", Project: "Facilitating the professional life of women without discrimination with the implementation of social timetables - Social timetable", programme Equal. (unp.)

Pillinger, J., 2000, "Working time in Europe: a European working time policy in the public services", E.T.U.I., Report 63, Brussels

Pillinger, J., 2002, " Work-life balance: a new politics of work and time", paper presented at the conference organised by the European Industrial Relations Review on *Work-life balance and diversity in European industrial relations,* London, June 21 & 22, 2002

POLITIS newspaper, 28/02/2006, page: 19. *Cyprus Mail* newspaper, "Gender wage gap among highest in EU" 8/3/2006.

Pfau-Effinger, Birgit. 2004. *Development of culture, welfare states and women's employment in Europe.* Aldershot, England; Burlington, VT: Ashgate.

Sisson, K.; Marginson, P. 2000, The impact of Economic and Monetary Union on industrial relations - A sectoral and company view. European Foundation for the Improvement of Living and Working Conditions Luxembourg : EUR-OP,

Soumeli, E., 2002, "Work-life balance issues in Greece", paper presented at the conference organised by the European Industrial Relations Review on *Work-life balance and diversity in European industrial relations,,* London, June 21 & 22.

Stoltz, Pauline. 1997. "Single mothers and the dilemmas of universal social policies [Denmark]." *Journal of Social Policy* 26(October):425-443.

U.S. Department of State. 2007. "Denmark: International Religious Freedom Report 2007.", 2008.

Symeonidou, H., Mitsopoulos, G. & K. Vezyrgianni, 2001, *The division of paid and unpaid work in Greece,* WORC, European Network on Policies and the Division of Unpaid and Paid Work

Third European Survey on Working Conditions, 2000, Foundation for the Improvement of Living and Working Conditions

Wahl A, Hook P., Holgersson C., & Linghag S. (2005), *"In order".* *Theories for Organization and Gender,* Gasouka M.(ed.), Athens: Research Centre for Equality Issues,

Weir, Bill and Sylvia Johnson. January 8, 2007. "Denmark: The Happiest Place on Earth." *ABC NEWS.* Retrieved 2/13/08 http://abcnews.go.com/print?id=4086092.

Zeis Th., Milioni F., (2005) eds. *Manual of Good Practices for Family-Work Balance,* National Theme Network for family-work balance, Athens: KETHI

Thoughts and Notes on the Issues of Reconciliation
of Work and Family Life in Europe.

163

Websites

www.alkistis-equal.gr

www.equal.gr

www.kethi.gr

www.koinoniko-orario.gr

www.dimosvoulas.gr

www.egaleo.gr

www.peristeri.gr

http://europa.eu/index_el.htm

www.pik@org.cy

www.elani.com.cy

www.bg.fnv.nl

http://www.comfia.net/acuerdo/index.htm#empresa

www.dti.gov.uk/work-lifebalance

www.familyfriendly.ie

www.fiba.it

www.ine.otoe.gr

www.tcd.ie/erc/servemploi

www.union-network.org

www.union-network.org/unisite/Groups/Women/Women.html

About the Authors

Maria Gasouka is an Assistant Professor at Aegean University in Greece where she teaches cultural and feminist subjects in the classroom and through distant learning at both a graduate and an undergraduate level. At the same time she is a researcher on Social Gender, Education and Labor Market. She is the author of 9 books and she has published numerous scientific articles in the Greek and English language. She is engaged as an expert in the designing, the implementation and the assessment of European Programmes and Union Initiatives and in this context she has recently cooperated with several Cypriot organizations of the public and private sector such as the Ministry of Justice, Labor and Education. She is the designer of the National Plan of Action for Gender Equality (2006-2013) of the Republic of Cyprus and President of the Scientific Committee of the Observatory for Equality in Cyprus (PIK).

Maria Kokkinou has studied Psychology (Bachelor's Degree) , Social Politics and Social Anthropology (Bachelor's Degree), Education (Master's Degree), Education and Migration (Doctor's Degree). She is the director of studies at a private school in Greece, a special educator and a psychologist working with young children and their families and a journalist. She is the author of 7 books. She has published articles in numerous national newspapers and magazines and she has been training high school teachers. She has done research on education, migration and social exclusion and recently she has been interested in research on gender equality.